The
WAR POETS

The WAR POETS

by Robert Giddings

BLOOMSBURY

First published in Great Britain 1988
by Bloomsbury Publishing Plc
38 Soho Square, London, W1V 5DF

This paperback edition first published 2000
Copyright © Toppan Printing Co. Ltd. 1988
Text copyright © Robert Giddings 1988
All rights reserved

A CIP record for this book can be obtained from The British Library.

ISBN 0 7475 4271 6

10 9 8 7 6 5 4 3 2 1

Typeset by Servis Filmsetting Ltd.
Printed in Singapore.

This book was edited, designed and produced by
The Paul Press Ltd.

Project Editor   Catherine Ellis
Art Editor   Lester Cheeseman
Editorial   Emma Warlow
Index   Dorothy Groves
Picture Researcher   Jane Lewis

Art Director   Stephen McCurdy
Editorial Director   Jeremy Harwood
Production Manager   Nicky Bowden

Half-title page: *"The Lost Chief"* (Punch)
Frontispiece: *Jonas "Le Guetteur"*
Title page: *"Listening Posts in the Snow"* (*Ernstes & Heiteres aus dem Wettkrieg*)
Contents: *"Through sloughs of despond: British artillery advancing through the
mud in Flanders"* (*The Great War, 12th January 1918*)

CONTENTS

INTRODUCTION

"I am determined that this war, with all its powers for devastation, shall not master my poeting; that is, if I am lucky enough to come through all right, I will not leave a corner of my consciousness covered up, but saturate myself with the strange and extraordinary new conditions of this life, and it will all refine itself into poetry later on."

Isaac Rosenberg, letter to Laurence Binyon, 1914

In 1936, 20 years after the Battle of the Somme, *The Oxford Book of Modern Verse 1892–1935* was published. It purported to be a collection of the finest poetry in our language produced in modern times. The editor was W. B. Yeats. He decided that the book should contain no poetry of the Great War 1914–18. In his *Introduction*, Yeats was quite candid about his decision to proscribe Owen, Sassoon, Graves and other war poets. He had a distaste for certain poems written during the war:

> *"In poems that had for a time considerable fame, written in the first person, they made suffering their own. I have rejected these poems for the same reason that made Arnold withdraw his* Empedocles on Etna *from circulation; passive suffering is not a theme for poetry. In all the great tragedies, tragedy is a joy to the man who dies; in Greece the tragic chorus danced . . .*
>
> *If war is necessary, or necessary in our time and place, it is best to forget its suffering as we do the discomforts of fever, remembering our comfort at midnight when our temperature fell."*

With a superior wave of his hand, Yeats dismisses such giants of 20th century literature as Owen, Graves, Sassoon, Blunden and a host of others who attempted to render the experience of 1914–18 in poetry. Yet, in all charity, we may make some effort to understand why Yeats found war poetry so difficult to accommodate. He was a victim of his own period and the limitations of his reading. There had been nothing like the poetry of the Great War before; there had been no war like the Great War. In the present day, the poets he so peevishly and grandly dismissed from his collection are considered to be among the greatest of modern poets, and his theory of poetry, of the appropriateness of particular subjects to poetic treatment and the avoidance of others, now seems affected. Yeats, however, simply could not accept what the poets of the Great War had to offer, his generation was quite unprepared. War had been a subject for poetry, but never like this.

There was hardly a year between the accession of Victoria and the outbreak of the Boer War when the British were not engaged in war overseas – in India, China, Africa, the Far East, the Near East, the Antipodes – but, significantly, not close to home in Europe. These were only 'little' wars, fought by professionals. Newspapers, popular entertainment and ephemera constantly steeped the Victorian consciousness in the idea of war as something irresistibly glamorous which happened a long way away.

Before 1914, when poets dealt with war it was to render it exotically or historically removed from immediate experience. War, in the hands of Macaulay, Tennyson, Arnold, Newbolt and Aytoun, had all the conviction of modern television costume drama. There were two outstanding exceptions – Rudyard Kipling and Thomas Hardy. Kipling made a serious attempt to reproduce the voice of the ordinary soldier and to get away from the bardic commentaries on the glories of the nation's victories. Even in his public statements such as *Recessional*, written for the Diamond Jubilee celebrations, his writing is shot through with a disquiet and unease that undercuts the proclaimed confidence of the moment it celebrates. Hardy wrote honestly and movingly about the Boer war, but most impressive is his epic treatment of the Napoleonic war, *The Dynasts*, which occupied him between 1904 and 1908. Though set a century in the past, *The Dynasts* strikes home with almost contemporary insight into the nature of wholesale international military conflict. In *Part 2* there is a description of the scene at Talavera that seems to foreshadow the whole mythology of Flanders.

Georgian poetry, which appeared just before the Great War, also found inspiration in the exotic, counterbalanced by romantic rhapsodizing about the English countryside. Both these aspects of Georgianism mythologized their subject matter, of which Flecker's "gorgeous East" and Brooke's Grantchester might be taken as two polarities. On the face of it, the generation which faced the catastrophe of 1914 was ill equipped poetically to express itself, having no tradition to draw upon, nor worthwhile models to imitate. At first, poets aped anthology pieces or relied on well established forms, but gradually the really original poets found their own voices.

In the version of literary history academically accepted until very recently, the doctrine was that there was a long lull during which little of value was created in English poetry, while the world waited for the revival of our genius in Modernism. This was the version of English literature in the 20th century which I was taught as an undergraduate. We can now see this for the pernicious nonsense that it is, in the just recognition of Graves, Sassoon, Brooke, Rosenberg and Owen, and the numerous – possibly lesser – poets who tried to portray the indescribable, and express the unthinkable during the years 1914–18. Yeats could not have been more mistaken. War is not necessary, but if it comes, then it is the poets' duty to make sure we never "forget its suffering, as we do the discomfort of fever, remembering our comfort at midnight when our temperature fell."

INTO BATTLE

1914

> *"War is a biological necessity of the first importance, a regulative element in the life of mankind which cannot be dispensed with . . . But it is not only a biological law but a moral obligation and, as such, an indispensible factor in civilization."*

Friedrich von Bernhard: *Germany and the Next War* (1912)

> *"It is the universal reign of Fear that has caused the system of alliances, believed to be a guarantee of peace, but now proved to be the cause of world-wide disaster . . . And this universal Fear has at last produced a cataclysm far greater than any of those which it was hoped to avert."*

Bertrand Russell: *War the Offspring of Fear* (1914)

One of the most striking facts about the Great War is the astonishing amount of poetry it inspired. Some of the finest English war poetry ever produced was written between 1914 and 1918. Keith Robbins makes this very clear in *The First World War*, giving an estimated number of war poems written in August 1914 as one and a half million—50,000 a day. It has become a tradition when assessing English poetry of the First World War to see a fairly clear division in the output of poetry. The claim is that the early poetry, written before the Battle of the Somme in 1916, was concerned with the struggle in a righteous cause and the chivalric and heroic aspect of military service, stressing the virtue of sacrifice and dwelling on the image of St. George of England versus the dragon of the Central Powers; and that the later poetry represents a sense of disillusionment brought on by involvement in a senseless war of attrition, and by the shattering cost of modern warfare in human terms. Julian Grenfell, Rupert Brooke, Robert Nichols and Charles Sorley are seen as the leading figures of the early war poetry, while Siegfried Sassoon, Wilfred Owen, Edmund Blunden and Isaac Rosenberg represent the second stage of the war. There is plenty of evidence to support this view, but signs of disquiet exist in much of the poetry written in the earliest days of the war.

POPULAR PATRIOTISM

The work of poets such as Henry Newbolt, Walter de la Mare and John Freeman accorded with popular patriotic sentiment at the beginning of the war, and John Masefield, with a touch of classic Georgian melancholy, reminded the brave young soldiers what it was they were fighting to preserve:

> "The harvest not yet won, the empty bin,
> The friendly horses taken from the stalls,
> The fallow on the hill not yet brought in,
> The cracks unplastered in the leaking walls,"

Yet, one of the greatest of the soldier-poets, Isaac Rosenberg, was already writing very uncompromisingly about the conflict. Rosenberg had gone to South Africa in June 1914 for the sake of his health and was enjoying considerable artistic and social success. He loathed the idea of the European conflict and wrote to Edward Marsh that he hoped the Kaiser "will have his bottom smacked—a naughty aggressive schoolboy who will have *all* the plum pudding". Although successful in Cape Town, he was not warmly received by the Jewish community and, as war fever developed, South Africa seemed less and less attractive. He had hoped to stay on and do a lot of work, returning to Europe with a large portfolio, but alas it was not to be. Removed from Europe by so many miles, distanced from his social contacts in London and his cultural and artistic roots, Rosenberg saw the terrible crisis in Europe with searing clarity. His poem, *On Receiving News of the War*, written in Cape Town, is one of the first really great poems of the First World War.

> "Snow is a strange white word.
> No ice or frost
> Has asked of bud or bird
> For Winter's cost.
>
> Yet ice and frost and snow
> From earth to sky
> This Summer land doth know.
> No man knows why.
>
> In all men's hearts it is.
> Some spirit old
> Hath turned with maligned kiss
> Our lives to mould.
>
> Red fangs have torn His face.
> God's blood is shed.
> He mourns from His lone place
> His children dead.
>
> O! ancient crimson curse!
> Corrode, consume.
> Give back this universe
> Its pristine bloom."

John Masefield.

Edward Marsh.

Edward Marsh, a civil servant of independent means who launched the now-renowned series of volumes *Georgian Poetry*, was a patron for many contemporary writers and artists. Rosenberg wrote to Marsh on 28th August 1914:

> *"It's a fearful nuisance, this war, I think the perfect place is at the Front—we'll starve or die of suspense anywhere else . . .*
>
> *By the time you get this the war will only just have begun, I'm afraid. Europe will have just stepped into its bath of blood. I will be waiting with beautiful drying towels of painted canvas and precious ointments to smear and heal the soul; and lovely music and poems. But I really hope to have a nice lot of pictures and poems by the time all is settled again, and Europe is repenting of her savageries."*

THE DAY WAR BROKE OUT

Rupert Brooke learned of the outbreak of war while at a music hall in Norfolk. In the middle of the advertised programme, there abruptly appeared a cinematographic reproduction of a hand drawing patriotic symbols:

> *"funny pictures of a soldier and a sailor (at the time I suppose dying in Belgium), a caricature of the Kaiser, greeted with a perfunctory hiss— nearly everyone sat silent. Then a scribbled message was shown: 'War declared with Austria 11.9.' There was a volley of quick, low handclapping—more a signal of recognition than anything else. Then we dispersed into Trafalgar Square and bought midnight war editions . . . In all these days I haven't been so near tears; there was such tragedy and dignity in the people . . . .*
>
> *If there's any good in anything I've done, it's made by the beauty and goodness of . . . a few I've known. All these people at the front who are fighting muddledly enough for some idea called England—it's some faint shadowing of goodness and loveliness they have in their hearts to die for."*

Some of the basic ideas which were so soon to find full and rich expression in *The Soldier* are plain to see here. He later elaborated on his feelings about the news of the beginning of the war in his essay *An Unusual Young Man*. The young man in question is on holiday in Cornwall (Brooke changed the location; he himself had been on holiday with friends in Norfolk). When he hears the news he goes out to climb a hill of gorse and sits alone, looking at the sea. His mind is filled with images and a sense of confusion and strain, the word "Germany" bringing a collection of vague thoughts to mind: the pompous middle-class vulgarity of the buildings in Berlin; the wide restfulness of Munich; the taste of beer; innumerable glittering cafés; Wagner's *Der Ring*; the swish of evening air on the face as one skis past the pines; nights of drinking, singing and laughter. He then suddenly realized that his

Bravo, Belgium!

thoughts were continually returning to two periods of his life—the days after the death of his mother, and the time of his first deep estrangement from one he loved:

> *"After a bit he understood this. Now, as then, his mind had been completely divided into two parts: the upper running about aimlessly from one half relevant thought to another, the lower unconscious half labouring with some profound and unknowable change. This feeling of ignorant helplessness linked him with those past crises . . . Something was growing in his heart, and he couldn't tell what. But as he thought 'England and Germany', the word 'England' seemed to flash like a line of foam. With a sudden tightening of his heart he realized that there might be a raid on the English coast. He didn't imagine any possibility of it succeeding, but only of enemies and warfare on English soil. The idea sickened him . . .*
>
> *His astonishment grew as the full flood of 'England' swept him on from thought to thought. He felt the triumphant helplessness of a lover. Grey, uneven little fields, and small, ancient hedges rushed before him, wild flowers, elms and beeches, gentleness, sedate houses of red brick, proudly unassuming, a countryside of rambling hills and friendly copses. He seemed to be raised high, looking down on a landscape compounded of the western view from the Cotswolds, and the Weald, and the high land in Wiltshire, and the Midlands seen from the hills above Prince's Risborough. And all this to the accompaniment of tunes heard long ago, an intolerable number of them being hymns . . . To his great disgust, the most commonplace sentiments found utterance in him. At the same time he was extraordinarily happy."*

RALLYING TO THE COLOURS

Brooke resolved to serve in the armed forces and for a time considered getting a commission in the army via the Territorials at Cambridge. Then, in September 1914, Winston Churchill offered him a commission in the Royal Naval Division, which was then being formed and in October he sailed with his division for Antwerp, which was under German attack. His letters reveal him as being taken up with a strange mixture of terror and excitement, which he tried to convey to Edward Marsh, as they moved nearer and nearer the action:

> *"We got to a place called Vieux Dieux . . . passing refugees and Belgian soldiers by millions. Every mile the noise got louder, immense explosions and detonations . . . five or six thousand British troops, a lot of Belgians, guns going through, transport-waggons, motor cyclists . . . staff officers . . . An extraordinary and thrilling confusion. As it grew dark the thunders increased, and the sky was lit by extraordinary glares. We were all given entrenching tools. Everybody looked worried."*

Brooke wrote to Russell Loines, a good friend in New York, on Christmas Day:

> *"I don't know if you heard of my trip to Antwerp. A queer picnic. They say we saved the Belgian army, and most of the valuable things in the town—stores and ammunition . . . However, we at last got away . . . Antwerp that night was like several different kinds of hell—the broken houses and dead horses lit up by an infernal glare. The refugees were the worst sight. The German policy of frightfulness has succeeded so well, that out of that city of half a million, when it was decided to surrender Antwerp, not ten thousand would stay . . . I'll never forget that white-faced, endless procession in the night . . . the old men crying, and the women with hard drawn faces."*

Brooke had been exposed to one reality of the war, but he cannot have appreciated the disparity between a soldier's lot at the Front and his poetic vision of the fighting man's patriotic courage. The war was still blazing at Christmas and had proved more costly than anyone could have predicted. The devastating losses on both sides and the horrific atrocities that were reported from the Front were beginning to shake British confidence. One instance of notorious German cruelty was the brutal massacre by firing squad of over 600 civilians at Dinant on 23rd August; the corpses identified included that of a child only three weeks old. Yet, at Christmas time, Brooke was to be found correcting the proofs of his five sonnets *1914*, anticipating the next stage of the game.

CHARLES SORLEY ENLISTS

Meanwhile in England, Charles Sorley, another early poet of the Great War, was impatiently waiting to be billeted to the Front. Sorley was a scholar at Marlborough College, where he excelled at debating, games, and in the O.T.C., before winning a place at University College, Oxford. His parents advised him to study abroad for a year before going up, so he travelled to Germany and became immersed in German culture. When war was declared, he returned to England immediately to enlist. After months of training and military routine that he hated, he was finally posted in May 1915, a 2nd Lieutenant in the Suffolk Regiment.

Sorley's poetry is of a very different style to Brooke's. In fact, Sorley severely criticized Brooke's *1914* sonnets, claiming that the poet was over-praised and obsessed with his own sacrifice: "He has clothed his attitudes in fine words: but he has taken the sentimental attitude". Sorley was influenced primarily by Hardy, Masefield, Ibsen, Goethe and Homer, and he was highly critical of the Late Victorians:

> *"The voice of our poets and men of letters is finely trained and sweet to hear; it teems with sharp saws and rich sentiment: it is a marvel of delicate technique: it pleases, it flatters, it charms, it soothes: it is a living lie."*

He was critical, too, of some of Hardy's more "public" poetry, but, interestingly enough, praised *The Dynasts* for its honesty and unremitting truth to events and human nature. His attachment to German culture and learning made it easy for him to distrust the shallow British patriotism which greeted the start of the war, but at the same time he was distressed by Germany's brutality. In September 1914 he wrote:

"For the joke of seeing an obviously just cause defeated, I hope Germany will win. It would do the world good and show that real faith is not that which says 'we must win for our cause is just', but that which says 'our cause is just: therefore we can disregard defeat'. All outlooks are at present material, and the unseen value of justice as justice, independent entirely of results, is forgotten. It is looked upon merely as an agent for winning battles."

THE CHANGING POETIC VOICE

Almost as soon as the war had started, a self-conscious new genre of "war poem" had emerged in which all the expected attitudes were contained in an acceptably "poetical" style. J.C. Squire wrote in the *New Statesman* on 26th September:

"What is wrong with most of these patriotic versifiers is that they start with a ready-made set of conceptions, of phrases, of words, and of rhymes, and turn out their works on a formula. Put England down as 'knightly', state her honour to be 'inviolate' and her spirit 'invulnerable', call her enemies 'perjured' and 'branded with the mark of Cain', refer to 'Trafalgar' (which has always done good service as a rhyme to 'war') summon the spirits of Drake and Grenville from the deep, introduce a 'thou' or two, and conclude with the assertion that God will defend the Right—and there's the formula for a poem."

The poetry Charles Sorley wrote in the early months of the war reveals the narrowness of this critical generalization. The force of his work foreshadows the sense of disillusionment that was to characterize the poetry of the later years. He was, it must be confessed, something of an exception to the rule since, for many young poets, Rupert Brooke epitomized poetic excellence. W.N. Hodgson was of the school of Brooke, whose poetry he admired. When war broke out, he enlisted immediately and served in the Devonshire Regiment. His poetry was very much in the spirit of Brooke's, and appeared in *The Spectator* and *Saturday Post*, two popular patriotic magazines.

Seeking inspiration from Brooke's work, however, did not pre-clude originality. Wilfrid Gibson was a very close friend of Brooke's and a member of Edward Marsh's circle too, but his war poetry has an unusual quality, written as it was from the point of view of the ordinary foot soldier (Gibson served as a private in the infantry). His was a voice from the ranks and his poetry lacks the declamatory, self-consciously chivalric quality of much of the early First World War period. Before the war his poetry had been concerned with the lives of industrial workers and village labourers, and the themes of his war poetry can be seen as an extension of these interests, capturing and rendering poignant the fleeting moments of experience:

> *"We ate our breakfast lying on our backs*
> *Because the shells were screeching overhead."*

THE WOMEN'S VOICE

Another perspective on the war that emerges in the early poetry is the prevalent tone of disgust and dismay as English optimism was eroded. Although their contribution has been largely neglected, women had their part to play in the poetry of the war too, as has been recognized in Catherine Reilly's fine anthology *Scars upon My Heart*. Alice Meynell was already well known as an essayist and poet when the war broke out. A friend of Coventry Patmore, Meredith and Tennyson, her poetry had originally been refined, pious and delicately Late Victorian, but by the time she wrote *Summer in England 1914*, there were some new stylistic developments. Her poetry reveals her as a tough, uncompromising observer of the modern world and critical of its ways. To her, the war represented the ultimate folly of modern times, and she contrasted it with the routine luxuriance of the world of nature:

> "—while this rose made round her cup,
>   The armies died convulsed. And when
> This chaste young silver sun went up
>   Softly, a thousand shattered men,
> One wet corruption, heaped the plain,
>   After a league-long throb of pain."

Her view was shared by two other talented women poets—Mary Webb and Marie Carmichael Stopes—and their voices united to decry the pitiful waste of the war.

Robert Ernest Vernède was an example of a fighting poet who demonstrated sympathy with the sentiments of these women in England. An established writer of French descent, he enlisted in September 1914 in the 19th Royal Fusiliers, to be commissioned in 1915 in the Rifle Brigade. His closest friend, F.G. Salter, who served with him, described how intense and positive was Vernède's hatred of the war:

> *"He hated the cruelty it inflicts, and denied it as a test of efficiency, but his feelings went beyond that: he loved ardently the things which war destroyed, the good human life of fellowship and adventure . . . To him it was a clear cut issue of right and wrong when Germany let loose this evil*

upon Europe . . . He was a poor man and enlistment meant for him the immediate cutting off of the greater part of his and his wife's livelihood . . . But he at once enlisted."

Vernède's early war poems are a direct and unaffected statement of his feelings about the conflict.

"THEY WENT WITH SONGS TO THE BATTLE"

On 21st September 1914, *The Times* published what was to become one of the most frequently celebrated poems to emerge from the war—Laurence Binyon's *For the Fallen*. Binyon, born in 1869 and educated at St. Paul's and Trinity College, Oxford, was employed at the British Museum in charge of oriental prints and drawings, and did not go to the Front himself until 1916 when he went as a Red Cross orderly. *For the Fallen* appeared at the time when the Battle of the Marne and the advance to the River Aisne were foremost in the public's mind.

Laurence Binyon.

"With proud thanksgiving, a mother for her children,
England mourns for her dead across the sea.
Flesh of her flesh they were, spirit of her spirit,
Fallen in the cause of the free.

Solemn the drums thrill: Death august and royal
Sings sorrow up into immortal spheres.
There is music in the midst of desolation
And a glory that shines upon our tears.

They went with songs to the battle, they were young,
Straight of limb, true of eye, steady and aglow.
They were staunch to the end against odds uncounted:
They fell with their faces to the foe.

They shall grow not old, as we that are left grow old:
Age shall not weary them, nor the years condemn.
At the going down of the sun and in the morning
We will remember them.

They mingle not with their laughing comrades again;
They sit no more at familiar tables of home;
They have no lot in our labour of the day-time;
They sleep beyond England's foam.

But where our desires are and our hopes profound,
Felt as a well-spring that is hidden from sight,
To the innermost heart of their own land they are known
As the stars are known to the Night;

"French and Russian they matter not,
A blow for a blow and a shot for a shot! . . .
We have one foe and one alone, England . . ."

As the stars that shall be bright when we are dust,
Moving in marches upon the heavenly plain;
As the stars that are starry in the time of our darkness,
To the end, to the end they remain."

This is a strangely effective poem, of which it would be true to say that the whole is greater than the sum of its parts. It consciously adopts a kind of "high seriousness" that would have pleased Matthew Arnold, and assumes a Shakespearian tone of voice—"Age shall not weary them, nor the years condemn"—which obviously echoes "Age cannot wither

"The central purpose of my life, the aim and end of it now, the thing God wants of me, is to get good at beating Germans . . ."

her, nor custom stale/Her infinite variety" (Antony and Cleopatra). The word order is reminiscent of the Authorised Version of the Bible: "They mingle not with their laughing comrades". The poem gradually grew in reputation as its sentiments became more and more appropriate to the scale of the nation's grief. Although beginning in the spirit of 1914 ("Fallen in the cause of the free"), the themes of the poem, as they develop, grow closer to the mood of 1918. It has, of course, become the standard cenotaph poem, quoted at all military funerals. Several lines from *For the Fallen* are carved by the entrance to the British Museum as a tribute to its staff who died in the Great War. Yet, considering that Binyon wrote it when the war was only eight weeks old, it is surprising that his poem should have struck home so hard that it was published in *The Times*, and became one of the best-known poems of 1914–18.

"BUSINESS AS USUAL"

As A.J.P. Taylor points out in *English History 1914–1945*, the nation's motto as the Great War opened was "business as usual". It was assumed that Britain could win the war with the armed forces as they existed at the time—it would all be over by Christmas. It was believed, in fact, that the British Navy would do most of what needed to be done. At first the even tenor of Britain's ways had hardly been ruffled: county cricket matches continued until the end of August, the government had no manpower survey prepared, and none of the raw material stocks necessary for the supply of war material had been accumulated. Mobilization, which started on the afternoon of 4th August, was on a small scale at first. The Expeditionary Force was to consist of six infantry divisions and a cavalry division. At first, 14 territorial divisions were considered to be enough to protect the nation from invasion, then it was resolved that two of the regular divisions should stay at home as well. Eventually, the 5th and 6th divisions were sent to France, and more inevitably followed.

> *"You are ordered abroad as a soldier of the King to help our French comrades against the invasion of a common enemy. You have to perform a task which will need your courage, your energy, your patience. Remember that the honour of the British Army depends on your individual conduct. It will be your duty not only to set an example of discipline and perfect steadiness under fire but also to maintain the most friendly relations with those whom you are helping in this struggle. In this new experience you may find temptations both in wine and women. You must entirely resist both temptations, and, while treating all women with perfect courtesy, you should avoid any intimacy. Do your duty bravely. Fear God. Honour the King."*

> *(Horatio Herbert Kitchener, Lord Kitchener, a message to the soldiers of the British Expeditionary Force, 1914, to be kept by each soldier in his active service pay-book.)*

Beguiling the tedium of the long wait in shell-swept
"loop-holed" trenches: British soldiers enjoying a game of
dominoes during the siege-battle of the Aisne.

As losses mounted, there was an inescapable need for endless numbers of young recruits. Up until the end of the Somme battle in 1916, the *Daily Telegraph* and *Morning Post* printed the names of all casualties but after the Somme (during which casualties varied between 1,000 and 5,000 a day), only the officers casualty lists were published. Understandably, attitudes at home changed as weeks turned into months, 1914 merged into 1915, and years went by. People grew to be more matter of fact about receiving news of death, as it became more and more of a seeming inevitability.

The cinema was an important means of conveying to those at home some idea of active service abroad. In the early years of the war, newsreels showed high jinks at camp, jolly sing-songs, and men playing football. It was not until after the Somme that the public saw actual footage of men going over the top and getting shot or wounded (although there is some controversy about the authenticity of this footage). When we read *For the Fallen* it is hard to believe that it was written before the endless casualty lists became an everyday sight. It is as if through prescience that Binyon makes his appeal for stoicism in the face of the terrible loss of human life.

THE END OF THE FIRST YEAR

It had been predicted that the war would be over by Christmas; instead, Christmas was spent in the trenches. Yet, in spite of the mutual hardship suffered by the soldiers of the opposing forces, there were moments of comradeship. On Christmas Day, by which time the Western Front stretched from Switzerland to the English Channel, the soldiers of the opposing armies at Rouges Bancs, west of Fromelles, united in an extraordinary act of fraternization. Lieutenant Sir E. Hulse, of the 2nd Battalion Scots Guards describes the scene:

> "I was surprised to hear a hell of a din going on and not a single man left in my trenches; they were completely denuded . . . I heard strains of Tipperary *floating down the breeze, swiftly followed by a tremendous burst of* Deutschland über Alles, *and saw to my amazement, not only a crowd of about 150 British and Germans at the halfway house . . . opposite my lines, but six or seven such crowds, all the way down our lines . . . and so we went on, singing everything from* Good King Wenceslas *down to the ordinary Tommies' song and ended up with* Auld Lang Syne, *which we all, English, Scots, Irish, Prussians, Wurtemburgers etc. joined in. It was absolutely astounding.*"

SONG: IN WARTIME

At the sound of the drum,
Out of their dens they come, they come,
The little poets we hoped were dumb,
The little poets we hoped were dead,
The poets who certainly haven't been read
Since heaven knows when, they come, they come,
At the sound of the drum, of the drum, drum, drum.

At the sound of the drum,
O Tommy, they've *all* begun to strum,
With a horrible tumty, tumty, tum;
And it's all about you, and the songs they sing
Are worse than the bullets' villainous "ping",
And they give you a pain in your tumty-tum,
At the sound of the drum, of the drum, drum, drum.

At the sound of the drum,
O Tommy, you know, if we haven't all come
To stand by your side in the hideous hum,
It isn't the horrors of war we fear,
The horrors of war we've got 'em here,
When the poets come on like waves, and *come*
At the sound of the drum, of the drum, drum, drum.

Anonymous

The Things that Matter,
Scene: Loos, during the September offensive.
Colonel Fitz-Shrapnel receives the following
message from G.H.Q.:
"Please let us know, as soon as possible,
the number of tins of raspberry jam issued
to you last Friday."

HAPPY IS ENGLAND NOW

There is not anything more wonderful
Than a great people moving towards the deep
Of an unguessed and unfeared future; nor
Is aught so dear of all held dear before
As the new passion stirring in their veins
When the destroying Dragon wakes from sleep.

Happy is England now, as never yet!
And though the sorrows of the slow days fret
Her faithfullest children, grief itself is proud.
Ev'n the warm beauty of this spring and summer
That turns to bitterness turns then to gladness
Since for this England the beloved ones died.

Happy is England in the brave that die
For wrongs not hers and wrongs so sternly hers;
Happy in those that give, give, and endure
The pain that never the new years may cure;
Happy in all her dark woods, green fields, towns,
Her hills and rivers and her chafing sea.

What'er was dear before is dearer now.
There's not a bird singing upon his bough
But sings the sweeter in our English ears:
There's not a nobleness of heart, hand, brain
But shines the purer; happiest is England now
In those that fight, and watch with pride and tears.

John Freeman

From
THE FOURTH OF AUGUST

Now in thy splendour go before us,
Spirit of England, ardent-eyed,
Enkindle this dear earth that bore us,
In the hour of peril purified.

The cares we hugged drop out of vision,
Our hearts with deeper thoughts dilate.
We step from days of sour division
Into the grandeur of our fate.

Laurence Binyon

BREAKFAST

We ate our breakfast lying on our backs
Because the shells were screeching overhead.
I bet a rasher to a loaf of bread
That Hull United would beat Halifax
When Jimmy Stainthorpe played full-back instead
Of Billy Bradford. Ginger raised his head
And cursed, and took the bet, and dropt back dead.
We ate our breakfast lying on our backs
Because the shells were screeching overhead.

Wilfrid Wilson Gibson

IN THE AMBULANCE

Two rows of cabbages,
Two of curly-greens,
Two rows of early peas,
Two of kidney-beans.

That's what he keeps muttering,
Making such a song,
Keeping other chaps awake
The whole night long.

Both his legs are shot away,
And his head is light,
So he keeps on muttering
All the blessed night:

Two rows of cabbages,
Two of curly-greens,
Two rows of early peas,
Two of kidney-beans.

Wilfrid Wilson Gibson

ENGLAND TO HER SONS

Sons of mine, I hear you thrilling
To the trumpet call of war;
Gird ye then, I give you freely
As I gave your sires before,
All the noblest of the children I in love and anguish bore.

Free in service, wise in justice,
Fearing but dishonour's breath;
Steeled to suffer uncomplaining
Loss and failure, pain and death;
Strong in faith that sees the issue and in hope that triumpheth.

Go, and may the God of battles
You in His good guidance keep:
And if He in wisdom giveth
Unto His beloved sleep,
I accept it nothing asking, save a little space to weep.

W. N. Hodgson

MAD

Neck-deep in mud,
He mowed and raved—
He who had braved
The field of blood—
And as a lad
Just out of school
Yelled—*April Fool!*
And laughed like mad.

Wilfrid Wilson Gibson

1914

I. PEACE

Now, God be thanked Who has matched us with His hour,
    And caught our youth, and wakened us from sleeping,
With hand made sure, clear eye, and sharpened power,
    To turn, as swimmers into cleanness leaping,
Glad from a world grown old and cold and weary,
    Leave the sick hearts that honour could not move,
And half-men, and their dirty songs and dreary,
    And all the little emptiness of love!

Oh! we, who have known shame, we have found release there,
    Where there's no ill, no grief, but sleep has mending,
    Naught broken save this body, lost but breath;
Nothing to shake the laughing heart's long peace there
    But only agony, and that has ending;
    And the worst friend and enemy is but Death.

II. SAFETY

Dear! of all happy in the hour, most blest
    He who has found our hid security,
Assured in the dark tides of the world at rest,
    And heard our word, "Who is so safe as we?"
We have found safety with all things undying,
    The winds, and morning, tears of men and mirth,
The deep night, and birds singing, and clouds flying,
    And sleep, and freedom, and the autumnal earth.
We have built a house that is not for Time's throwing.
    We have gained a peace unshaken by pain for ever.
War knows no power. Safe shall be my going,
    Secretly armed against all death's endeavour;
Safe though all safety's lost; safe where men fall;
And if these poor limbs die, safest of all.

III. THE DEAD

Blow out, you bugles, over the rich Dead!
    There's none of these so lonely and poor of old,
    But, dying, has made us rarer gifts than gold.
These laid the world away; poured out the red
Sweet wine of youth; gave up the years to be
    Of work and joy, and that unhoped serene,
    That men call age; and those who would have been,
Their sons, they gave, their immortality.

*"Now, God be thanked Who has matched
us with His hour,
And caught our youth, and wakened us
from sleeping, . . ."*

Blow, bugles, blow! They brought us, for our dearth,
    Holiness, lacked so long, and Love, and Pain.
Honour has come back, as a king, to earth,
    And paid his subjects with a royal wage;
And Nobleness walks in our ways again;
    And we have come into our heritage.

IV. THE DEAD

These hearts were woven of human joys and cares,
    Washed marvellously with sorrow, swift to mirth.
The years had given them kindness. Dawn was theirs,
    And sunset, and the colours of the earth.
These had seen movement, and heard music; known
    Slumber and waking; loved; gone proudly friended;
Felt the quick stir of wonder; sat alone;
    Touched flowers and furs and cheeks. All this is ended.

There are waters blown by changing winds to laughter
And lit by the rich skies, all day. And after,
    Frost, with a gesture, stays the waves that dance
And wandering loveliness. He leaves a white
    Unbroken glory, a gathered radiance,
A width, a shining peace, under the night.

Rupert Brooke.

V. THE SOLDIER

If I should die, think only this of me:
    That there's some corner of a foreign field
That is for ever England. There shall be
    In that rich earth a richer dust concealed;
A dust whom England bore, shaped, made aware,
    Gave, once, her flowers to love, her ways to roam,
A body of England's breathing English air,
    Washed by the rivers, blest by suns of home.

And think, this heart, all evil shed away,
    A pulse in the eternal mind, no less
    Gives somewhere back the thoughts by England given;
Her sights and sounds; dreams happy as her day;
    And laughter, learnt of friends; and gentleness,
In hearts at peace, under an English heaven.

Rupert Brooke

EPITAPH ON AN ARMY OF MERCENARIES

These, in the days when heaven was falling,
    The hour when earth's foundations fled,
Followed their mercenary calling
    And took their wages and are dead.

Their shoulders held the sky suspended;
    They stood, and earth's foundations stay;
What God abandoned, these defended,
    And saved the sum of things for pay.

A. E. Housman
(Written after the First Battle of Ypres 12th October to 11th
November 1914. The British press coverage at the time made
much of the distinction between the regular professional soldiers
and the volunteer forces.)

A.E. Housman.

1914

War broke: and now the Winter of the world
With perishing great darkness closes in.
The foul tornado, centred at Berlin,
Is over all the width of Europe whirled,
Rending the sails of progress. Rent or furled
Are all Art's ensigns. Verse wails. Now begin
Famines of thought and feeling. Love's wine's thin.
The grain of human Autumn rots, down-hurled.

For after Spring had bloomed in early Greece,
And Summer blazed her glory out with Rome,
An Autumn softly fell, a harvest home,
A slow grand age, and rich with all increase.
But now, for us, wild Winter, and the need
Of sowings for new Spring, and blood for seed.

Wilfred Owen

THE SCHOOLFELLOW

Our game was his but yesteryear;
    We wished him back; we could not know
The self-same hour we missed him here
    He led the line that broke the foe.

Blood-red behind our guarded posts
    Sank as of old the dying day;
The battle ceased; the mingled hosts
    Weary and cheery went their way:

"To-morrow well may bring," we said,
    "As fair a fight, as clear a sun."
Dear lad, before the word was sped,
    For evermore thy goal was won.

Henry Newbolt

LEAVING FOR THE FRONT

Before I die I must just find this rhyme.
Be quiet, my friends, and do not waste my time.

We're marching off in company with death.
I only wish my girl would hold her breath.

There's nothing wrong with me. I'm glad to leave.
Now mother's crying too. There's no reprieve.

And now look how the sun's begun to set.
A nice mass-grave is all that I shall get.

Once more the good old sunset's glowing red.
In thirteen days I'll probably be dead.

Alfred Lichtenstein
Trans. Patrick Bridgwater

AUGUST 1914

What in our lives is burnt
In the fire of this?
The heart's dear granary?
The much we shall miss?

Three lives hath one life—
Iron, honey, gold.
The gold, the honey gone—
Left is the hard and cold.

Iron are our lives
Molten right through our youth.
A burnt space through ripe fields
A fair mouth's broken tooth.

Isaac Rosenberg

Henry Newbolt.

FIELD AMBULANCE IN RETREAT
Via Dolorosa, Via Sacra

I

A straight flagged road, laid on the rough earth,
A causeway of stone from beautiful city to city,
Between the tall trees, the slender, delicate trees,
Through the flat green land, by plots of flowers, by black canals
    thick with heat.

II

The road-makers made it well
Of fine stone, strong for the feet of the oxen and of the great
    Flemish horses,
And for the high wagons piled with corn from the harvest.
And the labourers are few;
They and their quiet oxen stand aside and wait
By the long road loud with the passing of the guns, the rush of
    armoured cars, and the tramp of an army on the march
    forward to battle;
And, where the piled corn-wagons went, our dripping
    Ambulance carries home
Its red and white harvest from the fields.

III

The straight flagged road breaks into dust, into a thin white
    cloud, .
About the feet of a regiment driven back league by league,
Rifles at trail, and standards wrapped in black funeral cloths.
Unhasting, proud in retreat,
They smile as the Red Cross Ambulance rushes by.
(You know nothing of beauty and of desolation who have
    not seen
That smile of an army in retreat.)
They go: and our shining, beckoning danger goes with them,
And our joy in the harvests that we gathered in at nightfall
    in the fields;
And like an unloved hand laid on a beating heart
Our safety weighs us down.

Safety hard and strange; stranger and yet more hard
As, league after dying league, the beautiful, desolate Land
Falls back from the intolerable speed of an Ambulance in retreat
On the sacred, dolorous Way.

May Sinclair

TO GERMANY

You are blind like us. Your hurt no man designed,
And no man claimed the conquest of your land.
But gropers both through fields of thought confined
We stumble and we do not understand.
You only saw your future bigly planned,
And we, the tapering paths of our own mind,
And in each other's dearest ways we stand,
And hiss and hate. And the blind fight the blind.

When it is peace, then we may view again
With new-won eyes each other's truer form
And wonder. Grown more loving-kind and warm
We'll grasp firm hands and laugh at the old pain,
When it is peace. But until peace, the storm
The darkness and the thunder and the rain.

Charles Hamilton Sorley

"ALL THE HILLS AND VALES ALONG"

All the hills and vales along
Earth is bursting into song,
And the singers are the chaps
Who are going to die perhaps.
    O sing, marching men,
    Till the valleys ring again.
    Give your gladness to earth's keeping,
    So be glad, when you are sleeping.

Cast away regret and rue,
Think what you are marching to.
Little live, great pass.
Jesus Christ and Barabbas
Were found the same day.
This died, that went his way.
    So sing with joyful breath.
    For why, you are going to death.
    Teeming earth will surely store
    All the gladness that you pour.

Earth that never doubts nor fears,
Earth that knows of death, not tears,
Earth that bore with joyful ease
Hemlock for Socrates,
Earth that blossomed and was glad
'Neath the cross that Christ had,
Shall rejoice and blossom too
When the bullet reaches you.
    Wherefore, men marching
    On the road to death, sing!
    Pour your gladness on earth's head,
    So be merry, so be dead.

From the hills and valleys earth
Shouts back the sound of mirth,
Tramp of feet and lilt of song
Ringing all the road along.
All the music of their going,
Ringing swinging glad song-throwing,
Earth will echo still, when foot
Lies numb and voice mute.
    On, marching men, on
    To the gates of death with song.
    Sow your gladness for earth's reaping,
    So you may be glad, though sleeping.
    Strew your gladness on earth's bed,
    So be merry, so be dead.

Charles Hamilton Sorley

Charles Hamilton Sorley.

"WHEN YOU SEE MILLIONS OF THE MOUTHLESS DEAD"

When you see millions of the mouthless dead
Across your dreams in pale battalions go,
Say not soft things as other men have said,
That you'll remember. For you need not so.
Give them not praise. For, deaf, how should they know
It is not curses heaped on each gashed head?
Nor tears. Their blind eyes see not your tears flow.
Nor honour. It is easy to be dead.
Say only this, "They are dead." Then add thereto,
"Yet many a better one has died before."
Then, scanning all the o'ercrowded mass, should you
Perceive one face that you loved heretofore,
It is a spook. None wears the face you knew.
Great death has made all his for evermore.

Charles Hamilton Sorley

Right: *A gallant rescue under fire: this man saved twenty lives like this.*

DECAMPMENT

There was a time when fanfares
tugged bloodily at my impatient heart
and made it, prancing upwards like a horse,
seize its bit in fury.
At that time a march of drums
beat out the attack on every road,
and rain of bullets seemed to us
earth's most glorious music.
Then, suddenly, life halted.
Roads led between old trees.
Rooms enticed us.
It was sweet to rest, forget oneself,
unchain the body from reality
as from dusty armour,
bed voluptuously
quilted in mild dreamt hours.
But one morning through the misty air
rolled the echo of signals,
hard, sharp, whistling like sword-cuts.

It was as if through darkness suddenly lights gleamed.
It was as if through bivouacs at early morning
trumpet calls grated, sleeping men leapt up
and struck their tents, and horses were harnessed.
I was inserted into ranks that pushed into morning,
fire above helmets and stirrups.
Forward, into battle light blood
with tightened reins.
Perhaps at evening
victory marches would spread around us,
perhaps we would lie outstretched somewhere
among corpses.
But before the riving
and the foundering
our eyes would glow, drinking their fill
of world and sun.

Ernst Stadler
Trans. David McDuff

IN THE EAST

Like the wild organs of the winter storm
Is the people's gloomy rage,
The purple billow of battle
Of stars leaf-stripped.
With broken brows, silvery arms
The night beckons to dying soldiers.
In the autumnal ash-tree's shade
The ghosts of the killed are sighing.

Thorny wilderness surrounds the town.
From steps that bleed the moon
Drives off dumbfounded women.
Wild wolves have burst through the gate.

Georg Trakl
Trans. Michael Hamburger

LAMENT

Sleep and death, the dusky eagles
Around this head swoop all night long:
Eternity's icy wave
Would swallow the golden image
Of man; against horrible reefs
His purple body is shattered.
And the dark voice laments
Over the sea.
Sister of stormy sadness,
Look a timid dinghy goes down
Under stars,
The silent face of the night.

Georg Trakl
Trans. Michael Hamburger

GRODEK

At nightfall the autumn woods cry out
With deadly weapons, and the golden plains
The deep blue lakes, above which more darkly
Rolls the sun; the night embraces
Dying warriors, the wild lament
Of their broken mouths.
But quietly there in the pastureland
Red clouds in which an angry god resides,
The shed blood gathers, lunar coolness.
All the roads lead to blackest carrion.
Under golden twigs of the night and stars
The sister's shade now sways through the silent copse
To greet the ghosts of the heroes, the bleeding heads;
And softly the dark flutes of autumn sound in the reeds.
O prouder grief! You brazen altars,
Today a great pain feeds the hot flame of the spirit,
The grandsons yet unborn.

Georg Trakl
Trans. Michael Hamburger

TO THE UNITED STATES

Traitors have carried the word about
 That your hearts are cold with the doubt that kills.
Fools! As though you could sink to doubt;
 You—whom the name of freedom thrills!

They fear lest we plead with you by our blood
 To throb with England in this great fight,
Caring no whit if the cause be good,
 Crying—"It's England's, account it right."

Nay but that call would be vain indeed;
 Not thus do brothers to brothers speak.
We shall not plead with you—let them plead,
 Whose heel is set on the necks of the weak

Let them plead who have piled the dead
 League after league in that little land,
Whose hands with the blood of babes are red,
 Red—while they'd grasp you by the hand.

Let them plead, if for shame they dare,
 Whose honour is broke and their oaths forsworn—
We shall know by the blood we share
 The answer you cannot speak for scorn.

September, 1914
Robert Ernest Vernède

THE CALL

Lad, with the merry smile and the eyes
  Quick as a hawk's and clear as the day,
You, who have counted the game the prize,
  Here is the game of games to play.
  Never a goal—the captains say—
Matches the one that's needed now:
  Put the old blazer and cap away—
England's colours await your brow.

Man, with the square-set jaws and chin,
  Always, it seems, you have moved to your end
Sure of yourself, intent to win
  Fame and wealth and the power to bend—
  All that you've made you're called to spend,
All that you've sought you're asked to miss—
  What's ambition compared with this
That a man lay down his life for his friend?

Dreamer, oft in your glancing mind
  Brave with drinking the faerie brew,
You have smitten the ogres blind
  When the fair Princess cried out to you.
  Dreamer, what if your dreams are true?
Yonder's a bayonet, magical, since
  Him whom it strikes, the blade sinks through—
Take it and strike for England, Prince!

Friend with the face so hard and worn,
  The Devil and you have sometime met,
And now you curse the day you were born
  And want one boon of God—to forget.
  Ah, but I know, and yet—and yet—
I think, out there in the shrapnel spray,
  You shall stand up and not regret
The life that gave so splendid a day.

Lover of ease, you've lolled and forgot
  All the things that you meant to right;
Life has been soft for you, has it not?
  What offer does England make to-night?
  This—to toil and to march and to fight
As never you've dreamed since your life began;
  This—to carry the steel-swept height,
This—to know that you've played the man!

Brothers, brothers, the time is short,
  Nor soon again shall it so betide
That a man may pass from the common sort
  Sudden and stand by the heroes' side.
  Are there some that being named yet bide?
Hark once more to the clarion call—
  Sounded by him who deathless died—
"This day England expects you all."

Robert Ernest Vernède

BEYOND THE PALE
(After reading the French evidence of the German atrocities.)

As men who, in some hideous ju-ju place,
Having found a naked ape with brutish tread
Whom once they knew, before his reason fled,
Decent and sane, a white man of their race,
Will close their eyes in horror for a space—
Then for sheer pity's sake, with no word said,
Since no word may avail, will strike him dead
And strive thereafter to forget his face:
So with these ravening brutes that once were men
A loathing world has held awhile its hand
Unable to believe such things could be,
Now, lest such baseness should be seen again,
  Let it in mercy flame across their land
  And sweep them to oblivion utterly.

Robert Ernest Vernède

1915

"I don't know what is to be done. This isn't war."

Lord Kitchener

"It is my unshakable belief that the country to which God gave Luther, Goethe, Bach, Wagner, Moltke, Bismarck and my grandfather will yet be called upon to fulfil great tasks for the wellbeing of humanity."

Kaiser Wilhelm II, letter to Houston Stewart Chamberlain, 25th November 1915

A letter of Rupert Brooke's, written over the Christmas holiday 1914, gives a very interesting picture of the state of Britain as the New Year waited in the wings:

"England is remarkable. I wish I had the time to describe it . . . There are a few people who've been so anti-war before, or so superstitious of diplomacy, that they feel rather out of the national feeling. But it's astonishing to see how the "intellectuals" have taken on new jobs . . . Masefield drills hard in Hampstead, and told me, with some pride, a month ago, that he was a Corporal, and thought he was going to be promoted to Sergeant soon. Cornford is no longer the best Greek scholar in Cambridge. He recalled that he was a very good shot in his youth, and is now Sergeant-Instructor of Musketry . . . My brother is a 2nd Lieutenant in the Post Office Rifles . . . Gilbert Murray and Walter Raleigh rise at six every day to line hedgerows in the dark, and 'advance in rushes' across the Oxford meadows."

The spirit of enthusiastic optimism was still in the air, and Brooke's own naive emotions at this time speak volumes. At this stage in his training in the Naval Division, Brooke lamented in his letters the fact that more than half the country, as he believed, were apathetic about the war and "don't want to die. Which is odd. I've been praying for a German raid". He relished the prospect of battle and showed an increasing impatience with his training routine: "My mind's gone stupid with drill and arranging about other men's food. It's all good fun. I'm rather happy. I've a restful feeling that all's going well".

DEADLOCK ON THE WESTERN FRONT

But all was *not* going well. The contrast between Brooke's eagerness to enter into the fray and the reality of the fighting on the Front could not have been more marked. The situation on the Western Front as 1915 dawned was deadlock. The opposing forces faced each other in 500 miles of trenches, reaching from Switzerland to the English Channel, while the politicians and commanders canvassed the various strategic proposals for relieving the stalemate.

A major problem for the British was manpower, since reinforcements would not be available until the spring. The numbers of newly enlisted men in Kitchener's New Army in the opening weeks of the war had outstripped the authorities' ability to equip them with uniforms and weapons—many of the new regulars drilled in civvies and with broomsticks. British commanders anticipated 500,000 new troops joining the struggle on the Western Front, including Army Corps from Canada, Australia and New Zealand.

General Erich von Falkenhayn, Chief of the German General Staff, hoped to deliver a decisive blow in the west to ensure that these new Allied troops could not develop into a serious threat to Germany's war effort. He was diverted from this scheme by Hindenburg, Ludendorff

*In France military co-operation ensured quality
control in munitions factories.*

and the Kaiser, who insisted that he use his reserves to bring off a crucial victory against the Russian armies in East Prussia. The battle of Masuria on 27th February 1915 was a triumph for the German forces, and the same German troops were sent to support Austrian efforts in Galicia early in May, when the Russian lines were broken. Although a shot in the arm for the Central Powers' morale, the diversion of troops from the Western Front to Galicia took the pressure off the Allies.

WILLS'S CIGARETTES.

MARSHAL JOFFRE.

French strategy was dominated by the unambiguous policy of liberating the sacred soil of the homeland, now under the jackboot of the Teutonic invader, and pressing for an advance on the Rhine. For France, 1915 was to be the year of the big breakthrough, achieved as the result of engaging the enemy time and time again, and thus exhausting German reserves—*la guerre d'usure*. When the German army was exhausted, then would come the moment for the great French *coup*. General Joffre, the Commander-in-Chief, asserted "*Je les grignote*" ("I keep nibbling away at them"). His policy was full of contradictions, however. The big victory against the German fortifications that faced the Allies would require a massive build up of men and artillery. The only hope of prevailing against German lines lay in surprise. An accumulation of troops such as Joffre's plan demanded would deny this vital element and the attempt would fail. But the heart of the French nation was dedicated to the achievement of this coup.

ATTACK ON THE EASTERN FLANK

On 2nd January 1915, Lord Fisher, British First Sea Lord, received a communication from the Grand Duke Nicholas for a diversionary expedition to relieve Turkish pressure on the Russian armies in the Caucasus. The suggestion was enthusiastically welcomed by Churchill, who saw this as a means of draining the energy of the Central Powers. In the words of Liddell Hart:

> "The strategical solution was to go round the trench barrier. Its advocates ... argued that the enemy alliance should be viewed as a whole, and that modern developments had so changed conceptions of distance and powers of mobility, that a blow in some other theatre of war would correspond to the historic attack on an enemy's strategic flank."

Since Turkey had entered the war at the end of 1914, Russia had become completely isolated from war supplies and the European Allies. The First Lord of the Admiralty, Lord Fisher, seized upon the plan to restore the Mediterranean-Black Sea route to Russia through the Turkish straits, combining a relief force with an attack on the Turkish forces. The strategic value of this channel between the Aegean Sea and the Sea of Marmora to his aim of diverting German attention from the Western Front impressed Churchill to the extent that its capture became something of an obsession.

"Some borne on stretchers dreamed of home . . ."

Rupert Brooke was delighted when he learnt that he was to be among the force sent to the Dardanelles. For him the expedition had all the glamour of Homeric associations and the gorgeous Orient:

> *"Do you think perhaps the fort on the Asiatic corner will want quelling . . . and they'll make a sortie and meet us on the plains of Troy? . . . Shall we have a Hospital Base . . . on Lesbos? Will Hero's Tower crumble under 15″ guns? Will the sea be polyphloisbic and wine-dark and unvintageable? Shall I loot mosaics from St. Sophia, and Turkish delight, and carpets . . .?"*

He had never felt so happy in his life, or so much that his life had a firm purpose. On 28th February, the Naval Division sailed on the *Grantully Castle* from Avonmouth. On 18th March, the first Anglo-French naval attack on the Dardanelles failed; it was badly organized and the ships used were already obsolete. Brooke and his division arrived at Port Said on 27th March, ignorant of what lay ahead.

Brooke enjoyed three days' leave for sight-seeing, viewing the pyramids and the Sphinx, riding camels and shopping in the bazaars. Sir Ian Hamilton, commander of the Anglo-French army assisting the navy in forcing the Dardanelles, came to review the Naval Division on 3rd April, and offered Brooke a post on his staff. Hamilton wrote to Edward Marsh:

> *"I saw Rupert Brooke, lying down under a shelter, rather off colour, poor boy. He had got a touch of the sun the previous day. It was nothing, and essentially he was looking in first-class physical condition."*

Brooke declined the offer, preferring to serve with his own men. The last poem he wrote, known simply as *Fragment*, was written on board the troopship which took him to the Aegean.

They landed at the beautiful Aegean island of Scyros on 17th April. Arthur Asquith described it to his sister:

> *"This island is more mountainous than Lemnos, and more sparsely inhabited. It is like one great rock-garden of white and pinkish-white marble, with small red poppies and every sort of wildflower; in the gorges ilex, dwarf holly, and occasional groups of olives; and everywhere the smell of thyme (or is it sage? or wild mint?). Our men kill adders and have fun with big tortoises. The water near the shore, where the bottom is white marble, is more beautifully green and blue than I have seen it anywhere."*

"The thundering line of battle stands,
And in the air Death moans and sings; . . ."

AN ENGLISH DEMIGOD DIES

Here Rupert Brooke seemed well and happy, until Tuesday 20th April. A Divisional Field-Day was held that day and as soon as dinner was over he went to bed, complaining of pains in his back and neck. There was a swelling in his lip. By the next evening he had a temperature of 103°F. Next morning his condition had deteriorated further: the swelling had increased and acute blood-poisoning was diagnosed. He was moved to the French hospital ship, *Duguay-Trouin*, which was also at Scyros. He lapsed into a coma and died on 23rd April, traditionally Shakespeare's birthday and the name day of Britain's patron saint, St. George. He was buried the same evening in a remote and beautiful olive grove. They covered the grave with some great pieces of white marble which were lying there about and on the back of his cross the Greek interpreter wrote in pencil:

"Here lies the servant of God, sub-lieutenant in the English Navy, who died for the deliverance of Constantinople from the Turks."

Rupert Brooke had already begun to make his mark on the popular public memory of the Great War. On Easter Sunday, 4th April 1915, Dean Inge preached at St. Paul's Cathedral. After a man who vociferously protested against the war had been bundled out of the congregation, the Dean read Brooke's sonnet *"If I should die, think only this of me"*, and ventured to suggest that this young soldier should take rank with "our greatest poets". On 26th April Winston Churchill wrote in *The Times*:

"Rupert Brooke is dead. A telegram from the Admiral at Lemnos tells us that this little life has closed at the moment when it seemed to have reached its springtime. A voice had become audible, a note had been struck, more true, more thrilling, more able to do justice to the nobility of our youth in arms engaged in this present war, than any other . . . The voice has been swiftly stilled. Only the echoes and the memory remain; but they will linger.

During the last few months of his life, months of preparation in gallant comradeship in the open air, the poet-soldier told us with all the simple force of his genius the sorrow of youth about to die . . . He expected to die; he was willing to die for the dear England whose beauty and majesty he knew; and he advanced towards the brink in perfect serenity, with absolute conviction of the rightness of his country's cause, and a heart devoid of hate for fellow-men. . ."

Brooke had died without ever being engaged in battle, yet his death was hailed as *the* example of patriotic sacrifice. His romantic idealism remained intact until his death and his legacy is a collection of memorable poems that express a certain attitude to war which is as valid as it was in retrospect misplaced. It is not difficult to imagine how his beliefs would have faltered if he had lived longer, but it is futile to

The British bulldog wails aggressively
but sails impotently by – German view of the
British Dardanelles expedition.

speculate. The glamorous campaign in the Dardanelles whose prospect
had so thrilled him proved disastrous.

TRAGEDY AT GALLIPOLI

On 25th April, British troops began their landing at Gallipoli, together
with a force of Australian and New Zealand men, but Turkish resistance
was ferocious and the Allies made little headway. At Ari Burnu, the
Anzacs (Australian and New Zealand Army Corps) had losses of 5,000.
Again, on 6th August, the troops tried to press forward, but their
attempts were in vain and in October Gallipoli was evacuated. Allied
losses totalled 252,000.

Although time has vindicated Churchill's policy, and it is now
appreciated that the Dardanelles campaign was brilliantly conceived but
badly executed, Winston Churchill resigned from the Cabinet on 13th

November. He was made the scapegoat of the failure, but the root of the problem lay in the fact that so many ministers, including Kitchener, were more interested in successes on the Western Front.

IN THE TRENCHES

Here it was a story of little gain at enormous cost. The year opened with the Allied offensive in Artois and Champagne. This was an attempt by Joffre to free these areas of France from the Germans. Attacks along the western side of the Noyon salient and in the area between Reims and Verdun failed. The Germans retaliated along the La Bassé Canal and at Soissons, and the Allies counterattacked. The British made some headway at Neuve Chapelle in March, but the success was not followed up. Abortive assault followed assault and thousands of men died in the

Idealistic scenes like this were far removed from
the horrors of the typical clearing station.

process: the French casualties numbered 400,000. Today it is hard to appreciate fully the horrors of trench warfare that were endured from day to day.

Trench warfare on this scale was a totally new experience for both armies. From the northern border of Switzerland to the coastline near Ostend, the trenches stretched south-east to north-west over some 350 miles. This situation lasted from the winter of 1914 until the spring of 1918, and it has become an essential feature in our picture of the Great War—the image of those miles of trenches dominates all other memories. Major G.V. Carey of the Rifle Brigade and Captain H.S. Scott of the Royal Field Artillery, writing in *An Outline History of the Great War*, describe the amount of time and materials the Central Powers were able to exert on maintaining conditions in their defences and contrast this with the severe strain such maintenance placed on the Allies' efforts.

> *"In the British lines conditions were very different. The number of troops used to hold the crumbling trench system was excessive, as was the wastage from hardship and wounds. The autumn and winter rains of northern Europe are insistent. The digging of trenches even in the chalk of Artois is a bootless labour if materials for revetting, flooring and draining them are not to hand. In the loam of Flanders the front line trenches were in many places little more than ragged waterlogged ditches, and many of the communication trenches . . . were waistdeep in water."*

The condition of the trenches for the Allies was pitiable, over and above their exposure to enemy fire. The Germans soon realized that it was difficult to maintain continuous trenches and developed a defensive system of small concrete shelters—pill-boxes—and this system gradually replaced front line trenches. In the area immediately behind Allied lines the roads soon became worn out. The streets of the towns swam in inches of water and mud, fields were churned up by men and horses. In these conditions an infantry battalion might have a tour of duty of ten days which would include the maintenance of several miles of trenches —front line, support and communication—as well as carrying and transport duties, loading or delivering sacks of rations, mail, and stores under sniper fire and artillery bombardment.

Half the Allied line was occupied by the French. The British half of the line was populated by approximately 800 battalions of 1000 men in each, concentrated in two sectors—the Ypres Salient in Flanders and the Somme area in Picardy. Each had a ruined piece of public architecture which was to become its logo. Ypres had its famous Cloth Hall, and the Somme was symbolized by the basilica in the town of Albert; both these suffered gradual bombardment and destruction.

Ideally there should have been three lines of trenches. The front line trench, several hundred yards behind this the support trench line, and a similar distance behind that the reserve line. Trenches were of three kinds: firing trenches, like these three mentioned; communication trenches, which ran more or less perpendicularly to the line and connected the three trench lines; and the saps, which were shallow ditches projecting into No Man's Land and gave access to forward observation posts, listening posts, machine-gun positions and grenade-throwing posts. In addition there were the dug-outs—extra large holes excavated in the side of a trench for the use of one man. Some of these caverns housed ten or more soldiers and in their own crude way were often marvels of improvised engineering. It was in these mole-like conditions that thousands of troops spent their time at the Western Front. Edmund Blunden found a quality of antiquity at the Old British Line at Festubert, which had the appearance of great age and perpetuity:

> *"its weather-beaten sandbag wall was already venerable. It shared the past with the defences of Troy. The skulls which spades disturbed about it were in a manner coeval with those of the most distant wars."*

> (Undertones of War)

Others took a less classical view. George Coppard, for example, found the trenches above all shabby:

> *"The whole conduct of our trench warfare seemed to be based on the concept that we, the British, were not stopping in the trenches for long, but were tarrying a while on the way to Berlin and that very soon we would be chasing Jerry across country. The result, in the long term, meant that we lived a mean and impoverished sort of existence in lousy scratch holes."*

> (With a Machine Gun to Cambrai)

By contrast the German trenches epitomized enemy *gemütlichkeit* and thoroughness—they often had wooden floors, electric light, curtains, wallpaper, ceilings and comfortable furniture.

In *The New Church Times*, a section of the British troops' satiric paper *The Wipers Times*, in April 1916 these verses set the scene in the manner of the *Rubaiyat*:

"The passing whizz-bang shrieks and bullets hum
Yet, gentle stranger, to my dug-out come;
To you I'll unfold knowledge which may help,
But first methinks will ope a jar of rum.

This is a cheery place you will allow,
A tin of beef, a jar of rum, and Thou
Beside me, squatting in a pool of mud,
And dug-out is not Paradise enow.

And then! And then with five-nine crump you bet
The wily Hun burst up our parapet,
Blew off my roof, and made that blooming hole,
Through which you're now so quickly getting wet."

A NIGHTMARE OF ROUTINE

Robert Graves, serving with the Royal Welch Fusiliers in the British Expeditionary Force, had been introduced to the fearsome potential of modern weaponry when training in the O.T.C. at Charterhouse, but the theory became reality when he arrived at the Front, and he realized how far he had underestimated the suffering and terror that could be induced by war. His celebrated autobiography, *Goodbye To All That*, reveals the true nature of life in the trenches with unremitting candour. Graves describes the way in which routine almost eradicated the awfulness of the fighting—the damp, the rain, the lack of creature comforts, the unfairness and inhumanity of it all became almost submerged under the rhythm of army life. He brings the war so close that we can almost smell the foul trench air and hear the thunder of the guns:

> *"From the morning of September 24th to the night of October 3rd, I had in all eight hours of sleep. I kept myself awake and alive by drinking about a bottle of whisky a day . . . We had no blankets, greatcoats, or waterproof sheets, nor any time or material to build new shelters. The rain poured down. Every night we went out to fetch in the dead of the other battalions. The Germans continued indulgent and we had few casualties. After the first day or two the corpses swelled and stank. I vomited more than once while superintending the carrying. Those we could not get in from the German wire continued to swell until the wall of the stomach collapsed, either naturally or when punctured by a bullet; a disgusting smell would float across. The colour of the dead faces changed from white to yellow-grey, to red, to purple, to green, to black, to slimy."*

NEW THREATS

Worse was to come, however, as chlorine gas and submarines began to be deployed extensively by the Germans. At the second battle of Ypres between 22nd April and 25th May, the Germans attacked with a horrifying 5,000 cylinders of chlorine gas which prevented the Allies gaining any ground. Losses on all sides were high; the Germans lost 35,000, the British 60,000 and the French 10,000. The first British attempt to cripple the German lines with gas attacks was at Loos in the autumn. The attempt was a fiasco because the wind changed at a critical moment and blew the lethal gas back into British lines. Gas masks at this time were primitive to say the least, and the troops were devastated. The gas technicians went back to their drawing boards in despair. At huge cost—60,000 killed, missing or wounded—some little ground was gained, which had to be held at further cost. The failure of the British Expeditionary Force to gain any real advantage was blamed on their Commander-in-Chief, Sir John French, and he resigned in December to be replaced by Sir Douglas Haig. At home, the press proclaimed the brief campaign to be "A Great British Victory".

WILLS'S CIGARETTES.

FIELD-MARSHAL LORD FRENCH.

German U-boats were proving a significant threat in the waters around Britain. On 7th May, the *Lusitania* was sunk off the Irish coast, with the loss of 1198 lives. Of these, 139 were U.S. and war fever swept across the U.S.A. The New York correspondent of the *Daily Mail* reported the outrage:

> *"Like a prairie fire, indignation and the bitterest resentment is sweeping today over the American continent. The only question is: Will this universal feeling of horror and mingled grief for the innocent victims of the greatest crime in history overwhelm the government and force it into a declaration of war?"*

This terrible tragedy fuelled the propagandists' outcry against German atrocities but failed to draw the U.S.A. into the war immediately. The victimization of people with German or German-sounding names increased and England was incensed into aggressive patriotism.

THE HOME FRONT

On 1st February the Kaiser had authorized Zeppelin raids on London. Britain declared her blockade of Germany a month later. A German invasion of Britain was genuinely feared and on the east coast boats were taken in from the sea to prevent their use by the enemy. Pleasure piers, it was believed, might be used for landings and several of them were blown up. Barbed wire was coiled along the beaches. Basil Hallam, the music-hall artiste, was killed in active service this year. He had appeared in April 1914 at the Palace Theatre in *The Passing Show of 1914*, where he had sung "I'm Gilbert, the Filbert, the Knut with a 'K'"—Knuts (or Nuts) were the prototypical public school twits who made good at the Front. They wore monocles, carried bizarre firearms, sported very wide breeches and dazzling boots. This generation of "good sports" was more or less wiped out by the end of 1915.

All manner of persuasion was exerted to compel young men to the Front. Aquascutum, the sporting tailors, informed their staff:

> *"We think it is absolutely necessary for every single man between 19 and 30 to answer his country's call. We shall be pleased to pay half his present salary to any of our present employees while serving and will keep his situation open for him."*

Other firms simply dismissed staff in the hope they would do the decent thing and enlist. In the early months of the war the straight appeal to patriotism had been enough.

Baroness Orczy founded the Active Service League in which women had to sign a pledge that they would persuade every man they knew to volunteer for war service, and pledge never to be seen in public with any man fit enough to serve who was not in the forces. By 1915, the

"Pack up your troubles in your old kit bag,
And Smile, Smile, Smile!"

*Early war enthusiasm did not long
survive the first casualty lists.*

giving of white feathers had become a craze, following in the tradition of A.E.W. Mason's adventure novel, *The Four Feathers*, in which the hero is given four white feathers as a sign of cowardice and spends the rest of the novel in an epic struggle to return them to the people who gave them. It was particularly effective to give a white feather to the son of high class parents, suggesting that it was the born duty of all such to offer to die for their country. Compton Mackenzie believed that young women used these emblems to get rid of boyfriends they had tired of. Rosa Lewis of the Cavendish Hotel (the original of Evelyn Waugh's Lottie Crump in *Vile Bodies*), distributed white feathers indiscriminately, and her terrier was trained to bite the heels of any man not in uniform. Horatio Bottomley ran a thundering campaign in the pages of his journal, *John Bull*, and made numerous personal appearances as an evangelist of recruiting.

The darker side of the patriotic coin circulated by Bottomley and the vociferous jingoists was racial intolerance and national paranoia; "spymania" swept through the country like a disease. Shops run by those suspected of being German were subject to victimization. Herbert Asquith, the Prime Minister, eventually gave in to public pressure and ordained that enemy aliens should be interned. London Promenade Concerts were purged of music by Richard Strauss, Wagner and Beethoven. The Coburg Hotel, Mayfair, changed its name to The

Connaught. Anti-German feeling was whipped up by sensational stories of atrocities and cartoons in popular newspapers. As E.D. Morel wrote in *The Labour Leader* on 15th April 1915:

> "a systematic endeavour to represent your enemy . . . as outside the pale of human kind, is an absolute necessity today for any Government that has involved its people in war. It is only by such means that the willingness of millions of people who have nothing to gain and everything to lose by war can be induced to tolerate war. And so God and the humanities are alternately invoked to describe the enemy as a fiend among the nations, and fear and hatred act as chief recruiting sergeants."

THE POETIC VISION

The poetry that was written in this year represents an interesting combination of attitudes. In May, one of the key poems of the early stages of the war was published in *The Times*—Julian Grenfell's poem

"To-night I smell the battle; miles away
Gun-thunder leaps and thuds along the ridge; . . ."

"He stirred, shifting his body; then the pain
Leaped like a prowling beast, and gripped and tore
His groping dreams with grinding claws and fangs . . ."

Into Battle appeared in print on the day that his death was announced.

Into Battle is significant not because it is a great poem, but because it captures the curious rapture with which it was still possible to write about the war. Grenfell was a regular soldier who had been a member of the Eton-Balliol set fostered by Edward Marsh. In the Royal Dragoons, serving in India, he had enjoyed to the full all the activities considered appropriate to a young cavalry officer. In South Africa, where he was next stationed, he developed into a skilful boxer and horseman. He wrote to his family from Africa:

> "I love the profession of arms, and I love my fellow officers and all my dogs and all my horses."

Active service in 1914 excited him even further, he described war as a "big picnic" and from Flanders he wrote:

> "Here we are, in the burning centre of it all, and I would not be anywhere else for a million pounds and the Queen of Sheba . . . I have never, never felt so well, or so happy, or enjoyed anything so much. It just suits my stolid health, and stolid nerves, and barbaric disposition. The fighting-excitement vitalizes everything, every sight and word and action."

"Gas! GAS! Quick, boys! An ecstasy of fumbling,
Fitting the clumsy helmets just in time; . . ."

*"The whole conduct of our trench warfare seemed to be based on the
concept that we, the British, were not stopping in the trenches for long, . . ."*

Grenfell earned a reputation for bravery by stalking German snipers and then shooting them from very close range. He was twice mentioned in dispatches and awarded the Distinguished Service Order. Wounded in the head by a splinter from a shell near Ypres, Grenfell died in hospital at Boulogne. He had sent the poem home several weeks before he was killed.

"The naked earth is warm with Spring,
    And with green grass and bursting trees
Leans to the sun's gaze glorying,
    And quivers in the sunny breeze;

And life is colour and warmth and light,
    And a striving evermore for these;
And he is dead who will not fight;
    And who dies fighting has increase.

The fighting man shall from the sun
    Take warmth, and life from the glowing earth;
Speed with the light-foot winds to run,
    And with the trees to newer birth;
And find, when fighting shall be done,
    Great rest, and fullness after dearth.

Julian Grenfell.

All the bright company of Heaven
    Hold him in their high comradeship,
The Dog-Star, and the Sisters Seven,
    Orion's Belt and sworded hip.

The woodland trees that stand together,
    They stand to him each one a friend;
They gently speak in the windy weather;
    They guide to valley and ridge's end.

The kestrel hovering by day,
    And the little owls that call by night,
Bid him be swift and keen as they,
    As keen of ear, as swift of sight.

The blackbird sings to him, "Brother, brother,
    If this be the last song you shall sing,
Sing well, for you may not sing another;
    Brother, sing."

In dreary, doubtful waiting hours,
    Before the brazen frenzy starts,
The horses show him nobler powers;
    O patient eyes, courageous hearts!

And when the burning moment breaks,
    And all things else are out of mind,
And only joy of battle takes
    Him by the throat, and makes him blind,

Through joy and blindness he shall know,
    Not caring much to know, that still
Nor lead nor steel shall reach him, so
    That it be not the Destined Will.

The thundering line of battle stands,
    And in the air Death moans and sings;
But Day shall clasp him with strong hands,
    And Night shall fold him in soft wings."

Into Battle is a neutral poem. It is not about the rights and wrongs of the war, Germany's crime, or England's honour; it is an almost mystical celebration of man's need to struggle. Fighting is seen as the way human beings fulfil themselves, it is a manifestation of the life force itself, and if

"I saw him stab
And stab again
A well-killed Boche . . ."

the poem is read carefully it will be seen that throughout the fighting man is associated with the sun, the bright company of heaven and the world of nature. It is probable that 1915 was the last year in which such a war poem would be found acceptable by the British public.

POETS MOVE INTO BATTLE

1915 was also the year in which Edward Thomas, Isaac Rosenberg, Wilfred Owen, Ivor Gurney and David Jones enlisted—a wealth of poetic talent plunging into battle.

In the late summer of 1915, Edward Thomas enlisted as a private in the Artists' Rifles. Born on 3rd March 1878, the son of a civil servant in London, he was educated at St. Paul's School and Lincoln College,

Oxford, where he studied history. He described himself as a hack, and indeed his work as a book reviewer and author was prodigious even if the financial rewards were slight. His prose works show that characteristically Georgian love of the English countryside, but expressed by a first rate intelligence, and he wrote many books which rhapsodized the English landscape, as well as several outstanding literary critical works. He had been writing poetry since 1912, using the pen-name Edward Eastaway. He met Robert Frost when the American poet visited London and worked with Frost for about a year immediately prior to the Great War. He also wrote some excellent social journalism which catches the mood of the time brilliantly in an economic but colourful prose. But Thomas did not write his celebrated war poetry until he had been made an officer when, by and large, he was made financially secure. The relatively good money he was paid freed him from the hack work to which he had previously been enslaved in order to pay the bills. This unaccustomed economic ease was not to be his until 1916, when he had been trained as a map-reading instructor and served as a cadet in the Royal Artillery.

Isaac Rosenberg tried to join up at the end of October 1915. He was found to be physically fit, but too short for the infantry or the Royal Army Medical Corps. He was eventually recruited into the "Bantam" battalion which was to be part of the new 40th Division. The "Bantam" battalions were introduced so as to accommodate men who were too small to meet the requirements as to size and height in the army. He hoped to leave home without arousing his mother's suspicions, as he knew there would be very strong family objections to his joining the army, so he took only a comb and handkerchief with him, hoping that the British Army would provide the rest. He wrote to Edward Marsh:

> "I have just joined the Bantams and am down here amongst a horrible rabble. Falstaff's scarecrows were nothing to these. Three out of every four have been scavengers, the fourth is a ticket-of-leave. But that is nothing: though while I'm waiting for my kit I'm roughing it a bit, having come down here without even a towel. I dry myself with my pocket handkerchief . . . I meant to send you some poems I wrote which are better than my usual things, but I've left them at home where I am rather afraid to go for a while."

Wilfred Owen was teaching English in Bordeaux when the war broke out. He remained there until 1915, when he decided that teaching in France while the war continued would not bring him peace of mind. He first considered joining the French Army, and then enlisting in the Italian Cavalry (Italy had declared war on Germany on 23rd May), but in the end he resolved on the Artists' Rifles. He wrote to Leslie Gunston:

> "I don't imagine that the German War will be affected by my joining in, but I know my own future Peace will be."

On 12th August he received a package from his mother which contained *The Times* supplement of 10th August—*War Poems from The Times*. It included Thomas Hardy's *Song of the Soldiers*, Laurence Binyon's *For the Fallen*, Julian Grenfell's *Into Battle* as well as poems by Newbolt, Walter de la Mare and Bridges. He took this in his case as he boarded the Channel ferry to return to England. He was sworn in at the Headquarters of the Artists' Rifles in Duke's Road, London on 21st October 1915. Unlike Rosenberg, Wilfred Owen was an officer, and was well set up with a uniform, comfortable billet, mobility and sick leave after his inoculations; initially army life seemed to suit him.

Meanwhile Rosenberg was picked on for being a Jew and as a result of a bad fall in training spent some time in the camp hospital. He drew more and more on poetry to sustain him. He wrote to Edward Marsh:

> *"I believe in myself more as a poet than a painter; I think I get more depth into my writing. I have only taken Donne with me and don't feel for poetry much in this wretched place. There is not a book or paper here; we are not allowed to stir from the gate, have little to eat . . . and are utterly wretched."*

Yet this is the man who was to work up the horrifying experiences of war into the stuff of immortal poetry. His superiors noticed that although he was frequently clumsy and awkward, he was very intelligent and conscientious. He was offered promotion to Lance Corporal. He refused. It was one thing to enlist in the army to show solidarity with the cause, but it was quite another willingly to make oneself part of the system. He had four days wonderful leave at Christmas which he spent with his family. Before he went on leave he sent Edward Marsh a poem he had written, *Marching, (As Seen From the Left File).*

> "My eyes catch ruddy necks
> Sturdily pressed back—
> All a red brick moving glint.
> Like flaming pendulums, hands
> Swing across the khaki—
> Mustard-coloured khaki—
> To the automatic feet.
>
> We husband the ancient glory
> In these bared necks and hands.
> Not broke is the forge of Mars;
> But a subtler brain beats iron
> To shoe the hoofs of death
> (Who paws dynamic air now).
> Blind fingers loose an iron cloud
> To rain immortal darkness
> On strong eyes."

Ivor Gurney was a tailor's son, born in Gloucester on 28th August 1890, who was considerably influenced by his godfather, the Revd. Alfred Cheesman. He was educated as a chorister at King's School, Gloucester, and showed pronounced musical ability, eventually winning an Open Scholarship to the Royal College of Music. He was a brilliant student. Stanford himself said that of his students—who included Bliss, Ireland and Vaughan Williams—Gurney was the most brilliant, but he was unteachable. He was clearly very highly strung and the signs of mental instability, which were to become extremely serious in the early 1920's, began to show themselves when he was a student. At the same time as he began to develop an interest in setting poetry to music (notably five Elizabethan lyrics in 1912) he began to write verse himself. Gurney also developed into a perceptive critic. He was encouraged by his fellow Gloucestershireman, the poet F.W. Harvey.

The week-end away from the front: British officers and
men on leave from the trenches arriving at Victoria.

Gurney did not like Rupert Brooke's greatly admired sonnets of 1914:

> *"It seems to me that Rupert Brooke would not have improved with age, would not have broadened; his manner had become mannerism, both in rhythm and diction . . . Great poets, great creators are not much influenced by immediate events; those must sink in to the very foundations and be absorbed."*

He tried very hard to get himself into the army but was turned down in 1914 because his eyesight was not good. He was accepted in 1915 and joined the 2nd and 5th Gloucestershire Regiment. He wrote with terrifying honesty about these months:

> *"It is a better way to die; with these men, in such a cause: than the end which seemed near me and was so desirable only just over two years ago."*

His mental illness was not brought on by the war; he carried the seeds of it already and he must have sensed how near he was to the brink of insanity by 1912.

David Jones was the son of a printer, born in Brockley, Kent, in 1895. He studied at Camberwell School of Art 1909–14, and enlisted in the Royal Welch Fusiliers, serving with this regiment, which also included Robert Graves and Siegfried Sassoon in its strength, as a private on the Western Front from December 1915 until March 1918. An account of the experiences of an eye-witness in the British army serving in France from December 1915 to July 1916 is the basic material for one of the great masterpieces of British war poetry, his *In Parenthesis*, although it was not published until 1937.

David Jones admitted that he was greatly inspired by reading T.S. Eliot's *The Waste Land* and wrote *In Parenthesis* conscious of its influence. *In Parenthesis* is a mixture of prose and free verse, interlarded with echoes and scenes from previous wars portrayed in literature. It draws heavily on the impact of *Henry V*, *Morte D'Arthur* and Welsh legends and history. Although he is clearly attempting to write a poem about all wars, the most effective sections are those which put before us accounts of the conflict of 1914–18 as it affected the men who found themselves involved in it. Often the most impressive and moving parts of *In Parenthesis* are those sections which strain the least consciously towards the poetical, and consequently (to their advantage) read like soldiers' letters home written by poets.

PERCEPTIONS CHANGE

Charles Hamilton Sorley had always been another one of those who tried to see things as they really were, without his perceptions or representations being distorted by the film of custom. Early in the war (October 1914) he had written in a letter:

"Though everything is eclipsed at present except material values, it is something novel. But I don't know that it is really good for the nation. It makes people think too much of the visible virtues—bravery, endurance and the obvious forms of self-sacrifice, which are noticed and given their reward of praise. It's a time of the glorification of the second best."

As he began to see more of the war and to understand the reactions of those at home, influenced as people were by the way the war was portrayed in newspapers, he began very much to resent the stereotypes into which participants were divided—ordinary soldiers, and the clean-shaven young officers. He wrote home in July 1915:

"I hate the growing tendency to think that every man drops overboard his individuality between Folkestone and Boulogne, and becomes on landing either 'Tommy' with a character like a nice big fighting pet bear and an incurable yearning and whining for mouth-organs and cheap cigarettes: or the Young Officer with a face like a hero and a silly habit of giggling in the face of death."

By August 1915 he had been promoted to captain but remained absorbed by his writing. In a letter home he commented:

"You will notice that most of what I have written is as hurried and angular as the handwriting: written out at different times and dirty with my pocket: but I have had no time for the final touch nor seem likely to have for some time."

Time for revision was indeed denied him: he was shot in the head during the battle of Loos on 13th October 1915. His poems were found in his kit. His volume *Marlborough and Other Poems* was published in 1916 and went through four editions. Sorley was 20 years old.

AN ETERNAL MOTIF

On 6th December 1915 an anonymous poem, *In Flanders Fields*, was published in *Punch*. Written by John McCrae, a Canadian medical officer during the second battle of Ypres, it became the best known poem of the First World War, its images becoming part of the collective memory of the war. Its influence is perpetuated in the Annual Festival of Remembrance with its numerous poppies and the selling of poppies as a means of raising charitable funds for war disabled.

"In Flanders fields the poppies blow
Between the crosses, row on row
That mark our place; and in the sky
The larks, still bravely singing, fly
Scarce heard amid the guns below.

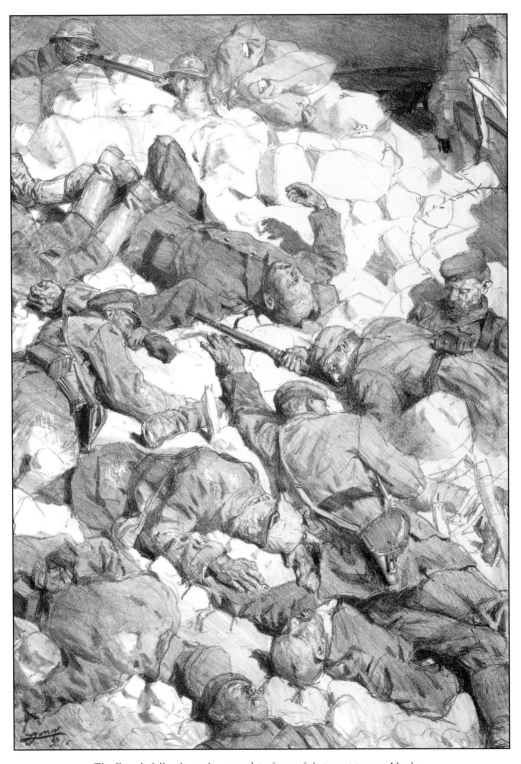

The French fallen litter the ground in front of their positions at Verdun.

We are the Dead. Short days ago
We lived, felt dawn, saw sunset glow,
    Loved and were loved, and now we lie
    In Flanders fields.

Take up our quarrel with the foe:
To you from failing hands we throw
    The torch; be yours to hold it high.
    If ye break faith with us who die
We shall not sleep, though poppies grow
    In Flanders fields.''

As Paul Fussell has pointed out in *The Great War and Modern Memory*, it manages to accumulate the maximum number of established motifs and images, which it mixes in a mood of autumnal pastoralism. Each image accurately triggers off its expected emotional response. We have the red flowers of traditional pastoral elegy—which go back to Milton (and beyond); the crosses which suggest the idea of Calvary and sacrifice; the sky as seen from a trench; the larks singing in the midst of the horrors and terrors of man's greatest folly; the contrast between the song of the larks and the voice of the guns; the special significance of dawn and sunset with the anticipated echoes of Gray's *Elegy*; the conception of soldiers as lovers; and the antithesis drawn between beds and graves. The poem sails across the imagination laden with literary associations ransacked from the riches of the past.

1915 was the first full year of war—a year which saw the casualty list of all the belligerents reach hitherto undreamed of heights. It also saw the end of the lingering remnants of chivalry that had been demonstrated as late as Christmas 1914, when, on the Western Front, British and German soldiers had mingled in No Man's Land. As 1916 was to show, war was now a brutal, unglamorous affair.

"Does it matter? – losing your sight? . . .
There's such splendid work for the blind;
And people will always be kind, . . ."

*"Here we are, in the burning centre of it all, and I would not be
anywhere else for a million pounds and the Queen of Sheba . . ."*

THE VOLUNTEER

Here lies a clerk who half his life had spent
Toiling at ledgers in a city grey,
Thinking that so his days would drift away
With no lance broken in life's tournament.
Yet ever 'twixt the books and his bright eyes
The gleaming eagles of the legions came,
And horsemen, charging under phantom skies,
Went thundering past beneath the oriflamme.

And now those waiting dreams are satisfied;
From twilight to the halls of dawn he went;
His lance is broken; but he lies content
With that high hour, in which he lived and died.
And falling thus he wants no recompense,
Who found his battle in the last resort:
Nor need he any hearse to bear him hence,
Who goes to join the men of Agincourt.

Herbert Asquith

IN TIME OF "THE BREAKING OF NATIONS"

I

Only a man harrowing clods
    In a slow silent walk
With an old horse that stumbles and nods
    Half asleep as they stalk.

II

Only thin smoke without flame
    From the heaps of couch-grass:
Yet this will go onward the same
    Though Dynasties pass.

III

Yonder a maid and her wight
    Come whispering by:
War's annals will fade into night
    Ere their story die.

Thomas Hardy

POSTCARD
(Sent to André Rouveyre, 20 August 1915)

I write to you beneath this tent
While summer day becomes a shade
And startling magnificent
Flowers of the cannonade
Stud the pale blue firmament
And before existing fade

Guillaume Apollinaire
Trans. Oliver Bernard

From RUPERT BROOKE

Your face was lifted to the golden sky
Ablaze beyond the black roofs of the square,
As flame on flame leapt, flourishing in air
Its tumult of red stars exultantly,
To the cold constellations dim and high;
And as we neared, the roaring ruddy flare
Kindled to gold your throat and brow and hair
Until you burned, a flame of ecstasy.

The golden head goes down into the night
Quenched in cold gloom—and yet again you stand
Beside me now with lifted face alight,
As, flame to flame, and fire to fire you burn . . .
Then, recollecting, laughingly you turn,
And look into my eyes and take my hand.

Wilfrid Wilson Gibson

Thomas Hardy.

MAY, 1915

Let us remember Spring will come again
　　To the scorched, blackened woods, where the
　　　wounded trees
Wait with their old wise patience for the heavenly rain,
Sure of the sky: sure of the sea to send its healing breeze,
　　Sure of the sun. And even as to these
　　　Surely the Spring, when God shall please,
　　Will come again like a divine surprise
To those who sit today with their great Dead, hands in their
　　hands, eyes in their eyes,
At one with Love, at one with Grief: blind to the scattered things
　　and changing skies.

Charlotte Mew

THE FALLING LEAVES
November 1915

Today, as I rode by,
I saw the brown leaves dropping from their tree
In a still afternoon,
When no wind whirled them whistling to the sky,
But thickly, silently,
They fell, like snowflakes wiping out the noon;
And wandered slowly thence
For thinking of a gallant multitude
Which now all withering lay,
Slain by no wind of age or pestilence,
But in their beauty strewed
Like snowflakes falling on the Flemish clay.

Margaret Postgate Cole

AN IMPERIAL ELEGY

Not one corner of a foreign field
But a span as wide as Europe;
An appearance of a titan's grave,
And the length thereof a thousand miles,
It crossed all Europe like a mystic road,
Or as the Spirits' Pathway lieth on the night.
And I heard a voice crying
This is the Path of Glory.

Wilfred Owen

SOCKS

Shining pins that dart and click
　　In the fireside's sheltered peace
Check the thoughts that cluster thick—
　　20 plain and then decrease.

He was brave—well, so was I—
　　Keen and merry, but his lip
Quivered when he said good-bye—
　　Purl the seam-stitch, purl and slip.

Never used to living rough,
　　Lots of things he'd got to learn;
Wonder if he's warm enough—
　　Knit 2, catch 2, knit 1, turn.

Hark! the paper-boys again!
　　Wish that shout could be suppressed;
Keeps one always on the strain—
　　Knit off 9, and slip the rest.

Wonder if he's fighting now,
　　What he's done an' where he's been;
He'll come out on top, somehow—
　　Slip 1, knit 2, purl 14.

Jessie Pope

TO VICTORY

Return to greet me, colours that were my joy,
Not in the woeful crimson of men slain,
But shining as a garden; come with the streaming
Banners of dawn and sundown after rain.

I want to fill my gaze with blue and silver,
Radiance through living roses, spires of green
Rising in young-limbed copse and lovely wood,
Where the hueless wind passes and cries unseen.

I am not sad; only I long for lustre,—
Tired of the greys and browns and the leafless ash.
I would have hours that move like a glitter of
        dancers
Far from the angry guns that boom and flash.

Return, musical, gay with blossom and fleetness,
Days when my sight shall be clear and my heart
        rejoice;
Come from the sea with breadth of approaching
        brightness,
When the blithe wind laughs on the hills with up-
        lifted voice

Siegfried Sassoon

VIGIL

A whole night long
crouched close
to one of our men
butchered
with his clenched
mouth
grinning at the full moon
with the congestion
of his hands
thrust right
into my silence
I've written
letters filled with love

I have never been
so
coupled to life

Giuseppe Ungaretti
Trans. Jonathan Griffin

GUARD-DUTY

A star frightens the steeple cross
a horse gasps smoke
iron clanks drowsily
mists spread
fears
staring shivering
shivering
cajoling
whispering
You!

August Stramm
Trans. Patrick Bridgwater

BATTLEFIELD

Yielding clod lulls iron off to sleep
bloods clot the patches where they oozed
rusts crumble
fleshes slime
sucking lusts around decay.
Murder on murder
blinks
in childish eyes.

August Stramm
Trans. Michael Hamburger

Germans in a trench on the Yser.

GONE, GONE AGAIN

Gone, gone again,
May, June, July,
And August gone,
Again gone by,

Not memorable
Save that I saw them go,
As past the empty quays
The rivers flow.

And now again,
In the harvest rain,
The Blenheim oranges
Fall grubby from the trees

As when I was young—
And when the lost one was here—
And when the war began
To turn young men to dung.

Look at the old house,
Outmoded, dignified,
Dark and untenanted,
With grass growing instead

Of the footsteps of life,
The friendliness, the strife;
In its beds have lain
Youth, love, age, and pain:

I am something like that;
Only I am not dead,
Still breathing and interested
In the house that is not dark:—

I am something like that:
Not one pane to reflect the sun,
For the schoolboys to throw at—
They have broken every one.

Edward Thomas

ONE NIGHT

I walked into a moon of gold last night,
Across grey sands she seemed to shine so bright.

Wide, wide the sands until I met the sea,
Cradle of moons, yet searchlights followed me.

I asked the moon if creeping round the Zones
She had seen good, or only poor things' bones.

"Pale faces I have seen, unconscious men
Bereft of struggling horror now and then.

"And sinking ships I see, and floating mines,
And cries I hear, 'O God', and choking whines.

"But later when the stars shine on the wave
And give more light, I know the dead die brave.

"Passing so quickly from the things that count,
Count to all mortal thoughts, to find the Fount,

"Where angels pour elixir into bowls,
Drink, not for broken hearts, but thirsty souls."

"And what on shore?" I asked, "the great Divide
Where rivers run, and trenches side by side?"

"There," the moon said, "the snow was on the ground
And the frost pinched me as I beamed around.

"Red pools of gore, and ghastly shadows lay
In deep dug corners, so I sank away.

"Let misty cloudlets sweep across my face
To hide the earth, and give me heart of grace.

"Sudden the air seemed filled with eager breath
Of great Adventurers, released from death,

"And shaking blood from out their eyes and hair
Shouting for further knowledge here and there.

"I lighted these across the treacherous Path
To reach the garden of Life's aftermath.

"And as they sped in troops the great guns boomed,
With flashes lightning swift, and dark hordes loomed,

"And phantom shapes of patient warrior bands—
Then more snow fell and shrouded all the lands."

Now pondering from the moon I turned again,
Over the sands, back to our House of Pain.

Millicent Sutherland

THIS IS NO CASE OF PETTY RIGHT OR WRONG

This is no case of petty right or wrong
That politicians or philosophers
Can judge. I hate not Germans, or grow hot
With love of Englishmen, to please newspapers.
Beside my hate for one fat patriot
My hatred of the Kaiser is love true:—
A kind of god he is, banging a gong.
But I have not to choose between the two,
Or between justice and injustice. Dinned
With war and argument I read no more
Than in the storm smoking along the wind
Athwart the wood. Two witches' cauldrons roar.
From one the weather shall rise clear and gay;

Out of the other an England beautiful
And like her mother that died yesterday.
Little I know or care if, being dull,
I shall miss something that historians
Can rake out of the ashes when perchance
The phoenix broods serene above their ken.
But with the best and meanest Englishmen
I am one in crying, God save England, lest
We lose what never slaves and cattle blessed.
The ages made her that made us from dust:
She is all we know and live by, and we trust
She is good and must endure, loving her so:
And as we love ourselves we hate her foe.

Edward Thomas

A PRIVATE

This ploughman dead in battle slept out of doors
Many a frozen night, and merrily
Answered staid drinkers, good bedmen, and all bores:
"At Mrs Greenland's Hawthorn Bush", said he,
"I slept." None knew which bush. Above the town,
Beyond "The Drover", a hundred spot the down
In Wiltshire. And where now at last he sleeps
More sound in France—that, too, he secret keeps.

Edward Thomas

Edward Thomas.

IN MEMORIAM (EASTER, 1915)

The flowers left thick at nightfall in the wood
This Eastertide call into mind the men,
Now far from home, who, with their sweethearts, should
Have gathered them and will do never again.

Edward Thomas

1916

"Perhaps the most extraordinary thing about a modern battlefield is the desolation and emptiness of it all . . . one cannot emphasize too much. Nothing is to be seen of war or soldiers—only the split and shattered trees and the burst of an occasional shell reveal anything of the truth. One can look for miles and see no human being. But in those miles of country (like moles or rats, it seems) lurk thousands, even hundreds of thousands of men, planning against each other perpetually some new device of death."

Harold Macmillan, serving with the Grenadier Guards, in a letter to his mother, 13th May 1916

"They advanced in line after line, dressed as if on parade, and not a man shirked going through the extremely heavy barrage, or facing the machine gun and rifle fire that finally wiped them out . . . the lines which advanced in such admirable order melted away under the fire. Yet not a man wavered, broke the ranks, or attempted to come back. I have never seen, indeed could never have imagined, such a magnificent display of gallantry, discipline and determination. The reports . . . from the very few survivors of this marvellous advance bear out . . . that hardly a man of ours got to the German front line."

Brigadier General Rees, General Officer commanding 94th Infantry Brigade, 31st Division, 1st July 1916

1916 was the year of the "big push". It was a year of continuing struggle at Verdun and of major confrontation on the Western Front at the Battle of the Somme. Although many argue that the Somme was a turning point in the war for the Allies, at the time it was a contentious strategy which certainly didn't succeed in its stated objective. Many of the war poets saw action at the Somme, and many lost their lives.

Edmund Blunden, who served with the Royal Sussex Regiment from 1915 and fought on the Somme, left brilliant descriptions of his experiences in his book *Undertones of War*. His account of the Somme battle is perhaps most impressive and memorable for the sense it gives of the chaos and confusion shared by those who take part in modern war, as compared with the crystal clear view of those commanders who plan the encounters, and as such it is a valuable supplement to a simple history of the war.

The Battle of the Somme was the brainchild of Douglas Haig, the new commander of the British Expeditionary Force. Haig had replaced

Sir John French in December 1915. He was a firm advocate of a major offensive as the way to victory, a belief that was buttressed by his faith in such Victorian military values as pluck, morale and stamina. In his view the Great War was only the Napoleonic Wars fought with modern weapons—a terrible misconception. His Staff College notes record this kind of attitude:

WILLS'S CIGARETTES.

FIELD-MARSHAL SIR D. HAIG.

> *"Modern arms of precision have no doubt been improved, but the human heart and pluck is just the same so that the hand which holds the arm of death trembles just as much or possibly more than in the old days."*

Controversy still rages about his ability and the results of his policy, but his thinking is clear: he attempted to apply the traditional principles he had learnt at Sandhurst to modern war.

Haig's problem was how to break through three lines of defence decisively. He favoured Napoleon's methods—the Advanced Guard strategy—in which the enemy was engaged on a wide front in order to locate his weak point, and then to bring up the General Reserve and push through it. Haig decided on a front of 100 miles, with the deployment of the Reserve after five or six days. This was the plan he was to follow at the Somme offensive.

The opening of 1916 saw France suffering serious shortages of manpower, a problem which was compounded in the early months by the struggle at Verdun. Attacks by German troops, and French counterattacks throughout May resulted in heavy losses on both sides. On the Eastern Front, after the Russian offensive at Vilna-Naroch in March which had resulted in huge casualties and collapse of the advance, the Russians rallied and launched a new offensive against the Austro-German lines. This forced Germany into a rapid deployment of troops from the Western Front and the Germans went on the defensive at the engagement at Verdun.

Although the crisis at Verdun had long delayed Haig's offensive, he now decided that Verdun had effectively performed the preparatory, wearing-down stage of his strategy and thus on 1st July, after a seven-day artillery bombardment, the British infantry on the Somme attacked the German Second Army along a 20 mile front. The resulting battle was to last until 15th November, but British gains were achieved at a huge cost. The advance was little more than eight miles, and Allied losses during those 20 weeks reached 600,000, two-thirds of whom were British. During the first day alone, British losses totalled 60,000, the largest number ever lost by the British army in a single day. Mud and barbed wire caused terrible problems, soldiers were exposed to machine gun fire during raids and attacks but, all told, the greatest killer was artillery which did not let up at all in the front zone.

The Germans had also suffered badly, however, although this was not fully appreciated by the Allies at the time. The most important fact about the German losses was the number of pre-war and non-commissioned officers who were killed. These experienced men were irreplaceable, and it was the consequences of this which have led many to argue that the Somme was the turning point for the Allies.

POETS AT THE FRONT

Early in January 1916 Isaac Rosenberg was transferred to Aldershot, where he joined the 12th South Lancashire Regiment. He found the food bad and the portions very small; it was his opinion that his survival depended on food parcels from home. In a run-down condition and suffering from a bad cold, he was assigned to coal shovelling fatigues. Only his growing reputation among his fellow soldiers for being a poet and artist sustained him. He found his companions rather frightening in the mood of potential violence they generated; brawling and drunkeness were commonplace. Rosenberg was in constant fear of being robbed or beaten. The weeding-out process which preceded service in France saved him, as most of the malcontents were posted out of his platoon as unfit for service.

Rosenberg himself was transferred to the 11th King's Own Royal Lancasters where he found the food better and the helpings more generous. He was further cheered by the news that his poem *Marching* was to be published in the U.S.A. (although it did not appear until December 1916). At the end of May the King came to inspect the regiment, prior to it being sent to France. On 29th May his regiment started for Southampton to embark on a ship to cross the Channel. He sketched himself on board and composed a poem on the experience of travelling on a troop ship:

> "Grotesque and queerly huddled
> Contortionists to twist
> The sleepy soul to a sleep.
> We lie all sorts of ways
> And cannot sleep.
> The wet wind is so cold,
> And the lurching men so careless,
> That, should you drop to a doze,
> Winds' fumble or men's feet
> Are on your face."

> (*The Troop Ship*)

Rosenberg was soon getting himself accustomed to life in the trenches. The heavy summer rains reached the Somme at the same time that the 40th Division (which included the King's Own Royal Lancasters) arrived. He wrote to a friend:

"I have been wet through for four days and nights . . . I lost all my socks and things before I left England, and hadn't the chance to make it up

"Halted against the shade of a last hill
They fed, and eased of pack-loads, were at ease; . . ."

again, so I've been in trouble, particularly with bad heels; you can't have the slightest conception of what such an apparently trivial thing means. We've had shells bursting two yards off, bullets whizzing all over the show, but all you are aware of is the agony of your heels."

A parcel from home soon supplied him with socks, underwear and other comforts—his mother had learned of Isaac's predicament and dealt with it immediately. He spent the year in the trenches in routine duties. It is from this period that dates *Break of Day in the Trenches*, one of his most famous poems.

"The darkness crumbles away—
It is the same old druid Time as ever.
Only a live thing leaps my hand—
A queer sardonic rat—
As I pull the parapet's poppy
To stick behind my ear.
Droll rat, they would shoot you if they knew
Your cosmopolitan sympathies.
Now you have touched this English hand
You will do the same to a German—
Soon, no doubt, if it be your pleasure
To cross the sleeping green between.
It seems you inwardly grin as you pass
Strong eyes, fine limbs, haughty athletes
Less chanced than you for life,
Bonds to the whims of murder,

> Sprawled in the bowels of the earth,
> The torn fields of France.
> What do you see in our eyes
> At the shrieking iron and flame
> Hurled through still heavens?
> What quaver—what heart aghast?
> Poppies whose roots are in man's veins
> Drop, and are ever dropping;
> But mine in my ear is safe,
> Just a little white with the dust."

Although miraculously Rosenberg's life was spared he was very close to the daily reality of death. He wrote to Edward Marsh on 17th August 1916:

> *"We had an exciting time today, and though this is behind the firing line . . . there were quite a good many sent to Heaven and the hospital. I carried one myself in a handcart to the hospital (which often is the antichamber (sic) to heaven)."*

Ivor Gurney was at this time serving as a private in the Gloucesters in France, nevertheless he carried on writing poems, composing songs and sending them back to England. His aim during his service abroad was simply to survive. His collection of verse *Severn and Somme*, published in 1917, contains several interesting poems which date from his military service in 1916 at the Lavantie-Fauquissart sector, between Béthune and Armentières. In July, Gurney was with the reserve for the Aubers Ridge offensive, and in the autumn his battalion was moved south to the Somme sector near Albert, at the front line of the Somme offensive. These early poems show Gurney not always avoiding the faults he had so clearly detected in Rupert Brooke. *To the Poet before Battle* is somewhat attitudinizing:

> "Now, youth, the hour of thy dread passion comes;
> The lovely things must all be laid away;
> And thou, as others, must face the riven day
> Unstirred by rattle of the rolling drums,
> Or bugles' strident cry. When mere noise numbs
> The sense of being, the fear-sick soul doth sway,
> Remember thy great craft's honour, that they may say
> Nothing in shame of poets. Then the crumbs
> Of praise the little versemen joyed to take
> Shall be forgotten; then they must know we are,
> For all our skill in words, equal in might
> And strong of mettle as those we honoured; make
> The name of poet terrible in just war,
> And like a crown of honour upon the fight."

At other times his honesty and close focus on the subject matter produce striking results, as in the short poem *Pain*:

"Pain, pain continual; pain unending;
Hard even to the roughest, but to those
Hungry for beauty . . . Not the wisest knows,
Nor most pitiful-hearted, what the wending
Of one hour's way meant. Grey monotony lending
Weight to the grey skies, grey mud where goes
An army of grey bedrenched scarecrows in rows
Careless at last of cruellest Fate-sending.
Seeing the pitiful eyes of men foredone,
Or horses shot, too tired merely to stir,
Dying in shell-holes both, slain by the mud.
Men broken, shrieking even to hear a gun.
Till pain grinds down, or lethargy numbs her,
The amazed heart cries angrily out on God."

Edward Thomas was rather luckier as in 1916 he was made a lieutenant in the Artists' Rifles and the increased pay he received enabled him to concentrate on his poetry. Although written at the front lines of the Somme, Thomas's poetry still shows the influence of the English countryside upon his creative imagination that gives his war poetry a particular poignance and edge. He often depicts scenes of rural life, or a casual conversation between passing neighbours, into which the idea of the war in Europe suddenly and distressingly intrudes.

"RENDEZVOUS WITH DEATH"

One of the most popular U.S. poets was killed at the Somme in 1916. Alan Seeger was born in New York in 1888 and spent much of his childhood in Mexico. He studied at Harvard, where he edited the *Harvard Monthly*. In 1912 he went to live in Paris and three weeks after the outbreak of the war he joined the French Foreign Legion, in company with about 40 other U.S. He fought at Champagne, where he was falsely reported to have been killed. He was awarded the Croix de Guerre and the Médaille Militaire. Then, at Belloy-en-Santerre on 4th July 1916, he and all his companions were mown down when six German machine gunners caught them in enfilade fire. This gave a particular resonance to his poem *Rendezvous*, which appeared in 1916 in *Collected Poems*.

The Somme claimed another poet, W.N. Hodgson, who was the son of the Bishop of St. Edmundsbury and Ipswich. Hodgson was born in 1893, educated at Durham and Christ Church, Oxford, and was influenced by Rupert Brooke. He was an outstanding athlete and volunteered for military service in the Devonshire Regiment on the outbreak of the war. In 1915 he was awarded the Military Cross. His poetry was published in *The Spectator*, and the *Saturday Post*, he also wrote some fine short stories. *Before Action* was written only two days before he was killed:

THE ANCHOR'S WEIGHED (1).
The tear fell gently from her eye,
    When last we parted on the shore;
My bosom heaved with many a sigh,
    To think I ne'er might see her more,
    To think I ne'er might see her more.

Mass-produced postcards concentrated on the sentimental idea of war, rather than its reality.

"By all the glories of the day
    And the cool evening's benison,
By that last sunset touch that lay
    Upon the hills when day was done,
By beauty lavishly outpoured
    And blessings carelessly received,
By all the days that I have lived
    Make me a soldier, Lord.

By all of man's hopes and fears,
    And all the wonders poets sing,
The laughter of unclouded years,
    And every sad and lovely thing;
By the romantic ages stored
    With high endeavour that was his,
By all his mad catastrophes
    Make me a man, O Lord.

I, that on my familiar hill
    Saw with uncomprehending eyes
A hundred of Thy sunsets spill
    Their fresh and sanguine sacrifice,
Ere the sun swings his noonday sword
    Must say goodbye to all of this;—
By all delights that I shall miss,
    Help me to die, O Lord."

Death continued to gather in his harvest and on 8th September 1916, T. Kettle, one of the most brilliant Irishmen of his generation, was killed. He was the son of a famous Irish land reformer and a friend of Padraic Pearse, the Irish nationalist and writer, leader of the Gaelic revival. Kettle was a lawyer and parliamentarian (M.P. for North-East Tyrone) and Professor of National Economics at University College, Dublin. When Belgium was invaded by the Germans, Kettle joined the Dublin Fusiliers—as an Irish nationalist he identified completely with the fate of a small oppressed nation, suffering at the hands of a ruthless occupying power.

Leslie Coulson was already a well known London journalist before the outbreak of war. He joined the 2nd Royal Fusiliers a month after the war started and served in Gallipoli, where he was wounded, and then in France. He was aged 27 when he was killed at the Somme on 7th October 1916. In the year after his death his volume of poetry, *From an Outpost and Other Poems*, sold over 10,000 copies.

A LITERARY FRIENDSHIP

Literary history can example some impressive friendships: Schiller and Goethe, Wordsworth and Coleridge. During the war many of the war poets met, and because of their poetry felt a special sympathy with each other. Robert Graves and Siegfried Sassoon had met in France in November 1915. Graves was visiting another mess and he noticed a copy of Lionel Johnson's *Essays* lying on a table. Apart from his own Keats and Blake it was the first book he'd seen in France that was not a trashy novel or a military textbook. Naturally his curiosity was aroused and he looked for a name on the flyleaf: it belonged to Siegfried Sassoon. As Graves records in *Goodbye to All That*, they were soon deep in conversation about poetry, and thus did two of the war's greatest poets meet at the officers' mess at 'C' Company, 1st Battalion, Royal Welch Fusiliers:

> "*Siegfried Sassoon had, at that time, published only a few privately-printed pastoral pieces of eighteen-ninetyish flavour, and a satire on Masefield which, half-way through, had forgotten to be a satire, and turned into rather good Masefield. We went to the cake shop and ate cream buns. At this time I was getting my first book of poems,* Over the Brazier, *ready for the press; I had one or two drafts in my pocket-book and showed them to Siegfried. He frowned and said that war should not be written about in such a realistic way. In return, he showed me some of his own poems. One of them began:*
>
> > '*Return to greet me, colours that were my joy,*
> > *Not in the woeful crimson of men slain*'
>
> *Siegfried had not yet been in the trenches. I told him, in my old-soldier manner, that he would soon change his style.*"

Robert Graves wrote to Edward Marsh that it was often quite difficult to talk to Sassoon about poetry because the other officers were terribly curious and suspicious:

> "*If I go into his mess and he wants to show me some new set of verses he says 'Afternoon, Graves, have a drink . . . by the way I want you to see my latest recipe for rum punch.' The trenches are worse than billets for privacy.*"

Sassoon had got to know Marsh through Edmund Gosse and early in 1916 he wrote to Marsh that he found Graves a strange person:

> "*full of ideas and originality. I am rather disappointed with his poems. Do you think it wise for him to publish them? I am sure he will do some much better work before long when he has recovered his balance.*"

In his fictionalized autobiography, *Memoirs of an Infantry Officer*, Sassoon has left a careful portrait of Robert Graves. Graves appears as David Cromlech, who is described as big and impulsive, with a "remarkable face, sallow, crooked and whimsical". Cromlech is an ideal companion, with disconcerting opinions and an expert at getting people's backs up unintentionally—"Far too fond of butting in with his own opinion before he'd been asked for it."

Sassoon was not the only person to notice this trait. Captain J.C. Dunn recorded in *The War the Infantry Knew 1914–1919—A Chronicle of Service in France and Belgium*, that Graves reputedly had the biggest feet in the British Army and seldom hesitated to put them into anything. Nevertheless, at this stage Graves and Sassoon (though they were later to drift apart) were good friends.

It is an odd fact that, although Graves was at this time preparing *Over the Brazier* for publication and went on to produce another volume of poems a year later (*Fairies and Fusiliers*), when he anthologized his own work for his collected verse he left out nearly all his war poetry. In June 1916 he wrote *The Last Post*:

> "The bugler sent a call of high romance—
> 'Lights out! Lights out!' to the deserted square:
> On the thin brazen notes he threw a prayer,
> 'God, if it's *this* for me next time in France . . .
> O spare the phantom bugle as I lie
> Dead in the gas and smoke and roar of guns,
> Dead in a row with the other broken ones
> Lying so stiff and still under the sky
> Jolly young Fusiliers, too good to die.'
> The music ceased, and the red sunset flare
> Was blood about his head as he stood there."

The year had brought both poets some pain. Sassoon broke his arm in a riding accident, and Graves had to have an operation on his nose—his septum had been displaced through boxing—in order to enable him to wear the new model of gas-helmet. This meant that he did not take part in the opening of the Somme offensive, which Sassoon recorded in his diary:

"*July 1, 7.30 a.m.*
Last night was cloudless and starry and still. The bombardment went on steadily. We had breakfast at 6. The morning is brilliantly fine, after a mist early. Since 6.30 there has been hell let loose. The air vibrates with incessant din—the whole earth shakes and rocks and throbs—in one continuous roar . . . Attack should be starting now, but one can't look out as the machine-gun bullets are skimming.
Inferno—inferno—bang—smash!
7.45 a.m. The artillery barrage is now working to the right of Fricourt and beyond. I have seen the 21st Division advancing on the left of Fricourt and

some Huns apparently surrendering—about three quarters of a mile away. Our men advancing steadily to the first line. A haze of smoke drifting across the landscape—brilliant sunshine. Some Yorkshires on our left (50th Brigade) watching the show and cheering as if at a football match."

This mood of optimism gradually darkened as the news of the losses and paltry gains arrived.

LAID LOW BY SHELLFIRE

Graves returned to active service on 5th July and was posted to the trenches at Givenchy. He fought in the area of Mametz Wood and the Bazentin High Wood. The Cameronians and the 5th Scottish Rifles led the attack, with the Royal Welch Fusiliers in reserve. Aware of the Royal Welch's position, the Germans began shelling them and Graves' battalion lost about a third of its men. Graves himself was badly wounded in the chest and thigh and, when his wounds had been dressed, he lay unconscious for more than 24 hours. In England his parents received conflicting reports: they heard that he had been wounded; then that he was "all right"; and then that he was recovering. They then had a letter from his commanding officer:

"I much regret to have to write and tell you your son has died of wounds. He was very gallant, and was doing so well and is a great loss. He was hit by a shell and very badly wounded, and died on the way down to the base I believe. He was not in bad pain . . . We have had a very hard time, and our casualties have been large. Believe me you have all our sympathy in your loss, and we have lost a very gallant soldier."

His parents received a telegram confirming his death; he was, of course, still alive and slowly recovering. Not long afterwards he was sent home to England.

Sassoon felt that something had died within himself. Looking back on the England he had known before the war he sensed that things would never be the same again. On 16th July he wrote:

"I'm thinking of England, and summer evenings after cricket-matches, and sunset above the tall trees, and village streets in the dusk, and the clatter of a brake driving home . . . So things went three years ago; and it's all dead and done with. I'll never be there again. If I'm lucky and get through alive, there's another sort of life waiting for me."

He admitted to himself that whenever he was in Graves' company he had the urge to do wild things, to travel, have adventures, write poetry: "anything but the old groove of cricket and hunting."

A GULF BETWEEN HOME AND WAR

Robert Graves was near breaking point; the war had emotionally and nervously exhausted him. He found it very difficult to talk to his parents and to put up with all the "war talk" in England.

When Graves returned home in August he found it very difficult to communicate with his parents. Unable to understand or share his feelings about the war, they on the other hand, were anxious to show him off to neighbours in his battle-stained officer's uniform. Having been coerced into going to church with them he sat there wondering why the vicar had not volunteered to serve in the army as he preached so eloquently about Divine Sacrifice and the glorious performance of our sons and brethren. Public opinion was vastly different from the sentiments of the men at the Front.

Britain had gone to war to help "plucky little Belgium", to drive the Boche back where they came from, but also, the war was to ensure that Germany would never again be in a position to threaten European peace. The defeat of Germany was the object of the war, the aim was total victory. Consequently, those who were not doing their bit for King and Country were slackers and shirkers. Up to 1916 the flow of volunteers had continued, but there was still a widespread belief that thousands were holding back. Late in 1915 conscription had been considered by the government, which had led to considerable tension in the House of Commons. Asquith produced a compromise, organized by Lord Derby, a scheme by which men of military age would "attest their willingness to serve" when called upon. No married man would be called upon to serve until all unmarried men had enlisted. This took the heat out of the political controversy, and appeased the various political parties.

CONSCRIPTION AND CONSCIENTIOUS
OBJECTORS

In January 1916, however, the first Military Service Act put an end to voluntary recruitment—unmarried men between the ages of 18 and 41 were now to be compelled to serve. Men who had a conscientious objection to military service had to prove their case before a tribunal, which had the power to grant them exemption. It was not really an efficient system, as tribunals tended to be unsympathetic, and matters of conscience are very hard to prove. Non-combatant service was granted to 7,000 objectors (usually ambulance work); 3,000 were sent to labour camps run by the Home Office; the remaining 1,500 absolutists (men who refused any form of compulsory service, on religious or political grounds), were drafted into military units, they could be court martialled if they disobeyed orders.

Conscription was not a great success. The Act produced 748,587 new claims of exemption. The average monthly enlistment after the Act seldom rose above 40,000—less than half the numbers obtained during

Ironic German comment on the Great Allied Offensive.

voluntary service. Feelings ran high and were whipped up in the press. Munition workers and coal miners were exempted from service, and for this many called them "shirkers". The war was to be won, it was claimed, not in the factories and coal mines, but at the Front. To solve the problem, universal military service for men up to the age of 41 was introduced on 26th April 1916.

Men such as Graves and Sassoon, who had seen the war at its most terrible, were distressed at some politicians' attitudes (Lloyd George proclaimed he would give the conscientious objectors a rough time—"I will make their path as hard as I can"), and by the military commanders' determination to continue the war to the bitter end. They found themselves alienated from public opinion.

POETS ON SICK LEAVE

While Graves was on leave, Sassoon was sent home with suspected lung trouble and the two enjoyed a holiday together—first at Harlech, then at Sassoon's family home in Kent. During Sassoon's period of sick leave, his friend "Robbie" Ross took him to Garsington Manor, near Oxford, to meet the celebrated Lady Ottoline Morrell who was married to Philip Morrell, a Liberal politician and pacifist, and supported several leading intellectuals and pacifists.

In November 1916, Graves and Sassoon rejoined their battalion at Litherland, near Liverpool. Soon after, Graves got himself pronounced fit for service overseas and returned to France. He was not really fully recovered but, as he told the doctor who examined him when he reached the 2nd Battalion near Bouchavesnes on the Somme, "I couldn't stand England any longer". During Christmas, while still in England, he had reflected on all the officers with whom he had spent Christmas 1915 but who were now dead:

> "I am more than twelve months older since then. 1916 has been a lucky year for me. This is a dreary flat place—fog and bleary sunsets and smoky munitions works at night with dotted lights and flares, and bugles blowing in the camp . . . and the intolerable boredom of mess and not enough work to do, and people waiting their turn to go out again. No one is at his best here . . . The year is dying of atrophy as far as I am concerned, bed-fast in its December fogs. And the war is settling down on everyone—a hopeless never-shifting burden. While newspapers and politicians yell and brandish their arms, and the dead rot in their French graves, and the maimed hobble about the streets."

There seemed to be no escape from his depression and torment, so he might as well go back to the trenches.

While Robert Graves was away, Sassoon was on his own and found he was able to work. *The March Past*, which he wrote that Christmas time, has a fine biting edge to it:

"Be slowly lifted up, thou long black arm,
Great Gun towering towards heaven, about to curse; . . ."

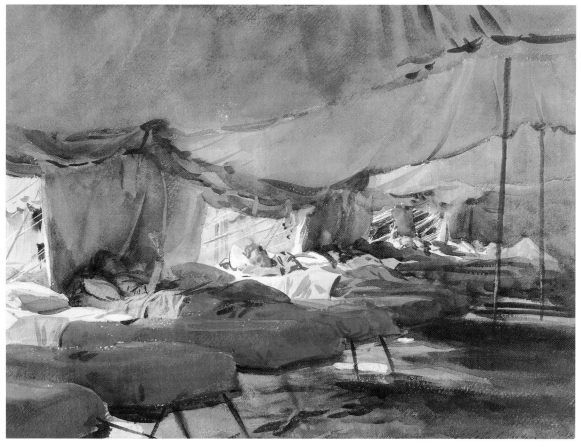

"Through gracious healing languors I can hear
Rumours of strife I need no longer share; . . ."

"In red and gold the Corps-Commander stood,
With ribboned breast puffed out for all to see:
He'd sworn to beat the Germans if he could;
For God had taught him strength and strategy.
He was our leader, and a judge of port—
Rode well to hounds, and was a damned good sort.

"Eyes right!" We passed him with a jaunty stare.
"Eyes front!" He'd watched his trusted legions go.
I wonder if he guessed how many there
Would get knocked out of time in next week's show.
"Eyes right!" The corpse-commander was a Mute;
And Death leered round him, taking our salute."

BITTERNESS AND DISILLUSION

The last gruelling fighting of the great Somme offensive of 1916 took place at the end of November. The first snow of the winter had begun to fall, the general feeling at the Front at the end of such a costly failure was one of bitterness and disillusion.

Robert Ernest Vernède served in the Rifle Brigade during the Somme campaign. When his commanding officer went sick, Vernède

Poincaré at Verdun tells Frenchmen
"Victory is ours".

was put in temporary command. On 1st September he was wounded in the thigh and sent home, but he returned to the Front in December, when he wrote *Before the Assault*:

"If thro' this roar o' the guns one prayer may reach Thee,
    Lord of all Life, whose mercies never sleep,
Not in our time, not now, Lord, we beseech Thee
    To grant us peace. The sword has bit too deep.

We may not rest. We hear the wail of mothers
    Mourning the sons who fill some nameless grave:
Past us, in dreams, the ghosts march of our brothers
    Who were most valiant . . . whom we could not save.

We may not rest. What though our eyes be holden,
    In sleep we see dear eyes yet wet with tears,
And locks that once were, oh, so fair and golden,
    Grown grey in hours more pitiless than years.

We see all fair things fouled—homes love's hands builded
    Shattered to dust beside their withered vines,
Shattered the towers that once Thy sunsets gilded,
    And Christ struck yet again within His shrines

Over them hangs the dust of death, beside them
    The dead lie countless—and the foe laughs still;
We may not rest, while those cruel mouths deride them,
    We, who were proud, yet could not work Thy will.

We have failed—we have been more weak than these
   betrayers—
In strength or in faith we have failed; our pride was vain.
How can we rest, who have not slain the slayers?
   What peace for us, who have seen Thy children slain?

Hark, the roar grows . . . the thunders reawaken—
   We ask one thing, Lord, only one thing now:
Hearts high as theirs, who went to death unshaken,
   Courage like theirs to make and keep their vow.

To stay not till these hosts whom mercies harden,
   Who know no glory save of sword and fire,
Find in our fire the splendour of Thy pardon,
   Meet from our steel the mercy they desire . . .

Then to our children there shall be no handing
   Of fates so vain—of passions so abhorr'd . . .
But Peace . . . the Peace which passeth understanding . . .
   Not in our time . . . but in their time, O Lord."

GERMANY OFFERS PEACE

In December 1916, there were several developments on the political
front which were to cast a different complexion on the new year. On 3rd
December, Robert Nivelle succeeded Joffre as French Commander-in-
Chief. On the 7th, Lloyd George became British Prime Minister of the
coalition government. Lloyd George did not have much confidence in
Haig, and found him a difficult character; Nivelle, on the other hand, he
found much more appealing. Consequently, Lloyd George agreed to the
subordination of British armies to Nivelle's authority—a decision
which was to have unfortunate repercussions, not the least of which was
a crisis in the relationship between British politicians and British
military commanders.

The general situation was one of deadlock on every front, with the
German blockade at sea beginning to make itself felt, and revolution
brewing in Russia. Woodrow Wilson had suggested peace, but without
success. On 12th December, the Germans put out feelers for peace,
indicating that they were prepared to negotiate, but their terms, which
were those of a victor to a vanquished foe, were unacceptable to the
Allies. Whatever the feelings of disillusion in the trenches, the British
Government, representing the general mood in Britain, was set on
winning the war and was not ready to sue for peace. Germany's treachery
to Belgium (which it now proposed to treat as a prize of war) could not be
forgotten. The peace feelers were rejected, and the war dragged on.

LAMPLIGHT

We planned to shake the world together, you and I
Being young, and very wise;
Now in the light of the green shaded lamp
Almost I see your eyes
Light with the old gay laughter; you and I
Dreamed greatly of an Empire in those days,
Setting our feet upon laborious ways,
And all you asked of fame
Was crossed swords in the Army List,
My Dear, against your name.

We planned a great Empire together, you and I,
Bound only by the sea;
Now in the quiet of a chill Winter's night
Your voice comes hushed to me
Full of forgotten memories: you and I
Dreamed great dreams of our future in those days,
Setting our feet on undiscovered ways,
And all I asked of fame
A scarlet cross on my breast, my Dear,
For the swords by your name.

We shall never shake the world together, you and I,
For you gave your life away;
And I think my heart was broken by the war,
Since on a summer day
You took the road we never spoke of: you and I
Dreamed greatly of an Empire in those days;
You set your feet upon the Western ways
And have no need of fame—
There's a scarlet cross on my breast, my Dear,
And a torn cross with your name.

May Wedderburn Cannan

PERHAPS . . .
To R.A.L.

Perhaps some day the sun will shine again,
And I shall see that still the skies are blue,
And feel once more I do not live in vain,
Although bereft of You.

Perhaps the golden meadows at my feet
Will make the sunny hours of spring seem gay,
And I shall find the white May-blossoms sweet,
Though You have passed away.

Perhaps the summer woods will shimmer bright,
And crimson roses once again be fair,
And autumn harvest fields a rich delight,
Although You are not there.

But though kind Time may many joys renew,
There is one greatest joy I shall not know
Again, because my heart for loss of You
Was broken, long ago.

Vera Brittain

THE VETERAN
May, 1916

We came upon him sitting in the sun,
    Blinded by war, and left. And past the fence
There came young soldiers from the Hand and Flower,
    Asking advice of his experience.

And he said this, and that, and told them tales,
    And all the nightmares of each empty head
Blew into air; then, hearing us beside,
    "Poor chaps, how'd they know what it's like?" he said

And we stood there, and watched him as he sat,
    Turning his sockets where they went away,
Until it came to one of us to ask
    "And you're—how old?"
                "Nineteen, the third of May."

Margaret Postgate Cole

"HARDEN OLD HEART . . ."

Harden old heart listen to the piercing cries
That the wounded in agony utter a long way off
O men lice of the earth tenacious vermin

Guillaume Apollinaire
Trans. Oliver Bernard

THE ANCRE AT HAMEL: AFTERWARDS

Where tongues were loud and hearts were light
    I heard the Ancre flow;
Waking oft at the mid of night
    I heard the Ancre flow.

I heard it crying, that sad rill,
    Below the painful ridge
By the burnt unraftered mill
    And the relic of a bridge.

And could this sighing river seem
    To call me far away,
And its pale word dismiss as dream
    The voices of to-day?
The voices in the bright room chilled
    And that mourned on alone;
The silence of the full moon filled
    With the brook's troubling tone.

The struggling Ancre had no part
    In these new hours of mine,
And yet its stream ran through my heart;
    I heard it grieve and pine,
As if its rainy tortured blood
    Had swirled into my own,
When by its battered bank I stood
    And shared its wounded moan.

Edmund Blunden

1916 SEEN FROM 1921

Tired with dull grief, grown old before my day,
I sit in solitude and only hear
Long silent laughters, murmurings of dismay,
The lost intensities of hope and fear;
In those old marshes yet the rifles lie,
On the thin breastwork flutter the grey rags,
The very books I read are there—and I
Dead as the men I loved, wait while life drags
Its wounded length from those sad streets of war
Into green places here, that were my own;
But now what once was mine is mine no more,
I seek such neighbours here and I find none.
With such strong gentleness and tireless will
Those ruined houses seared themselves in me,
Passionate I look for their dumb story still,
And the charred stub outspeaks the living tree.

I rise up at the singing of a bird
And scarcely knowing slink along the lane,
I dare not give a soul a look or word
Where all have homes and none's at home in vain:
Deep red the rose burned in the grim redoubt,
The self-sown wheat around was like a flood,
In the hot path the lizard lolled time out,
The saints in broken shrines were bright as blood.

Sweet Mary's shrine between the sycamores!
There we would go, my friend of friends and I,
And snatch long moments from the grudging wars,
Whose dark made light intense to see them by.
Shrewd bit the morning fog, the whining shots
Spun from the wrangling wire; then in warm swoon
The sun hushed all but the cool orchard plots,
We crept in the tall grass and slept till noon.

Edmund Blunden

WOMEN AT MUNITION MAKING

Their hands should minister unto the flame of life,
　　Their fingers guide
The rosy teat, swelling with milk,
To the eager mouth of the suckling babe
Or smooth with tenderness,
　　Softly and soothingly,
The heated brow of the ailing child.
Or stray among the curls
Of the boy or girl, thrilling to mother love.
　　But now,
Their hands, their fingers
Are coarsened in munition factories.
Their thoughts, which should fly
Like bees among the sweetest mind flowers,
Gaining nourishment for the thoughts to be,
Are bruised against the law,
　　"Kill, kill".
They must take part in defacing and destroying the natural body
Which, certainly during this dispensation
Is the shrine of the spirit.
　　O God!
Throughout the ages we have seen,
　　Again and again
　　Men by Thee created
　　Cancelling each other.
And we have marvelled at the seeming annihilation
　　Of Thy work.
But this goes further,
　　Taints the fountain head,
Mounts like a poison to the Creator's very heart.
　　O God!
Must It anew be sacrificed on earth?

Mary Gabrielle Collins

TO HIS LOVE

He's gone, and all our plans
　Are useless indeed.
We'll walk no more on Cotswold
　Where the sheep feed
　Quietly and take no heed.

His body that was so quick
　Is not as you
Knew it, on Severn river
　Under the blue
　Driving our small boat through.

You would not know him now . . .
　But still he died
Nobly, so cover him over
　With violets of pride
　Purple from Severn side.

Cover him, cover him soon!
　And with thick-set
Masses of memoried flowers—
　Hide that red wet
　Thing I must somehow forget.

Ivor Gurney

LAMENT

We who are left, how shall we look again
Happily on the sun or feel the rain
Without remembering how they who went
Ungrudgingly and spent
Their lives for us loved, too, the sun and rain?

A bird among the rain-wet lilac sings—
But we, how shall we turn to little things
And listen to the birds and winds and streams
Made holy by their dreams,
Nor feel the heart-break in the heart of things?

Wilfrid Wilson Gibson

AT THE MOVIES

They swing across the screen in brave array,
    Long British columns grinding the dark grass.
Twelve months ago they marched into the grey
    Of battle; yet again behold them pass!

One lifts his dusty cap; his hair is bright;
    I meet his eyes, eager and young and bold.
The picture quivers into ghostly white;
    Then I remember, and my heart grows cold!

Florence Ripley Mastin

GOLIATH AND DAVID
(For D.C.T., killed at Fricourt, March 1916)

Once an earlier David took
Smooth pebbles from the brook;
Out between the lines he went
To that one-sided tournament,
A shepherd boy who stood out fine
And young to fight a Philistine
Clad all in brazen mail. He swears
That he's killed lions, he's killed bears,
And those that scorn the God of Zion
Shall perish so like bear or lion.
But . . . the historian of that fight
Had not the heart to tell it right.

Robert Graves.

Striding within javelin range
Goliath marvels at this strange
Goodly-faced boy so proud of strength.
David's clear eye measures the length;
With hand thrust back, he cramps one knee,
Poises a moment thoughtfully,
And hurls with a long vengeful swing.
The pebble, humming from the sling
Like a wild bee, flies a sure line
For the forehead of the Philistine;
Then . . . but there comes a brazen clink
And quicker than a man can think
Goliath's shield parries each cast.
Clang! clang! and clang! was David's last
Scorn blazes in the Giant's eye,
Towering unhurt six cubits high.
Says foolish David, "Damn your shield!
And damn my sling! but I'll not yield."

He takes his staff of Mamre oak,
A knotted shepherd-staff that's broke
The skull of many a wolf and fox
Come filching lambs from Jesse's flocks.
Loud laughs Goliath, and that laugh
Can scatter chariots like blown chaff
To rout: but David, calm and brave,
Holds his ground, for God will save.
Steel crosses wood, a flash, and oh!
Shame for Beauty's overthrow!
(God's eyes are dim, His ears are shut.)
One cruel backhand sabre cut—
"I'm hit! I'm killed!" young David cries,
Throws blindly forward, chokes . . . and dies.
And look, spike-helmeted, grey, grim,
Goliath straddles over him.

Robert Graves

CASUALTY

They are bringing him down,
He looks at me wanly.
The bandages are brown,
Brown with mud, red only—
But how deep a red! in the breast of the shirt,
Deepening red too, as each whistling breath
Is drawn with the suck of a slow-filling squirt
While waxen cheeks waste to the pallor of death.
O my comrade!
My comrade that you could rest
Your tired body on mine, that your head might be laid
Fallen and heavy—upon this my breast,
That I might take your hands in my hands
To chafe! That abandoned your body might sink
Upon mine, which here helplessly, grievously stands;
That your body might drink
Warmth from my body, strength from my veins,
Life from my heart that monstrously beats,
Beats, beats and strains
After you vainly!
The trench curves. They are gone.
The steep rain teems down.
O my companion!
Who were you? How did you come,
Looking so wanly upon me? I know—
And O, how immensely long I have known—
Those aching eyes, numb face, gradual gloom,
That depth without groan!
Take now my love—this love which alone
I can give you—and shed without pain—
That life if I could I would succour,
Even as it were
This, this, my poor own!

Robert Nichols

THE DESERTER

There was a man,—don't mind his name,
Whom Fear had dogged by night and day.
He could not face the German guns
And so he turned and ran away.
Just that—he turned and ran away,
But who can judge him, you or I?
God makes a man of flesh and blood
Who yearns to live and not to die.
And this man when he feared to die
Was scared as any frightened child,
His knees were shaking under him,
His breath came fast, his eyes were wild.
I've seen a hare with eyes as wild,
With throbbing heart and sobbing breath.
But oh! it shames one's soul to see
A man in abject fear of death.
But fear had gripped him, so had death;
His number had gone up that day,
They might not heed his frightened eyes,
They shot him when the dawn was grey.
Blindfolded, when the dawn was grey,
He stood there in a place apart,
The shots rang out and down he fell,
An English bullet in his heart.
An English bullet in his heart!
But here's the irony of life,—
His mother thinks he fought and fell
A hero, foremost in the strife.
So she goes proudly; to the strife
Her best, her hero son she gave.
O well for her she does not know
He lies in a deserter's grave.

Winifred M. Letts

THE REFUGEES

Mute figures with bowed heads
They travel along the road:
Old women, incredibly old
and a hand-cart of chattels.

They do not weep:
their eyes are too raw for tears.

Past them have hastened
processions of retreating gunteams
baggage wagons and swift horsemen.
Now they struggle along
with the rearguard of a broken army.

We shall hold the enemy towards nightfall
and they will move
mutely into the dark behind us,
only the creaking cart
disturbing their sorrowful serenity.

Herbert Read

"Of them who running on that last high place
Breasted the surf of bullets, . . ."

A MEMORY

There was no sound at all, no crying in the village,
    Nothing you would count as sound, that is, after the shells;
Only behind a wall the low sobbing of women,
    The creaking of a door, a lost dog—nothing else.

Silence which might be felt, no pity in the silence,
    Horrible, soft like blood, down all the blood-stained ways;
In the middle of the street two corpses lie unburied,
    And a bayoneted woman stares in the market-place.

Humble and ruined folk—for these no pride of conquest,
    Their only prayer: "O! Lord, give us our daily bread!"
Not by the battle fires, the shrapnel are we haunted;
    Who shall deliver us from the memory of these dead?

Margaret Sackville

RENDEZVOUS

I have a rendezvous with Death
At some disputed barricade,
When Spring comes back with rustling shade
And apple-blossoms fill the air—
I have a rendezvous with Death
When Spring brings back blue days and fair.

It may be he shall take my hand
And lead me into his dark land
And close my eyes and quench my breath—
It may be I shall pass him still.
I have a rendezvous with Death
On some scarred slope of battered hill,
When Spring comes round again this year
And the first meadow-flowers appear.

God knows 'twere better to be deep
Pillowed in silk and scented down,
Where love throbs out in blissful sleep,
Pulse nigh to pulse, and breath to breath,
Where hushed awakenings are dear . . .
But I've a rendezvous with Death
At midnight in some flaming town,
When Spring trips north again this year,
And I to my pledged word am true,
I shall not fail that rendezvous.

Alan Seeger

"THE RANK STENCH OF THOSE BODIES HAUNTS ME STILL"

The rank stench of those bodies haunts me still,
And I remember things I'd best forget.
For now we've marched to a green, trenchless land
Twelve miles from battering guns: along the grass
Brown lines of tents are hives for snoring men;
Wide, radiant water sways the floating sky
Below dark, shivering trees. And living-clean
Comes back with thoughts of home and hours of sleep.

To-night I smell the battle; miles away
Gun-thunder leaps and thuds along the ridge;
The spouting shells dig pits in fields of death,
And wounded men, are moaning in the woods.
If any friend be there whom I have loved,
    speed
God (send) him safe to England with a gash.

It's sundown in the camp; some youngster laughs,
Lifting his mug and drinking health to all
     come
Who (came) unscathed from that unpitying waste:—
(Terror and ruin lurk behind his gaze.)
Another sits with tranquil, musing face,
Puffing his pipe and dreaming of the girl
       letter
Whose last scrawled (sheets) lies upon his knee.
The sunlight falls, low-ruddy from the west,
      heads; last week
Upon their (martial hair;) they might have died;
And now they stretch their limbs in tired content.

        Bosche has
One says "The bloody (Bosches have) got the knock;
"And soon they'll crumple up and chuck their games.
"We've got the beggars on the run at last!"

Then I remembered someone that I'd seen
    a
Dead in (the) squalid, miserable ditch,
Heedless of toiling feet that trod him down.

He was a Prussian with a decent face,
Young, fresh, and pleasant, so I dare to say.
No doubt he loathed the war and longed for peace,
And cursed our souls because we'd killed his friends.

Siegfried Sassoon.

THE KISS

To these I turn, in these I trust;
Brother Lead and Sister Steel.
To his blind power I make appeal;
I guard her beauty clean from rust.

He spins and burns and loves the air,
And splits a skull to win my praise;
But up the nobly marching days
She glitters naked, cold and fair.

Sweet Sister, grant your soldier this;
That in good fury he may feel
The body where he sets his heel
Quail from your downward darting kiss.

Siegfried Sassoon

One night he yawned along a half-dug trench
Midnight; and then the British guns began
With heavy shrapnel bursting low, and 'hows'
Whistling to cut the wire with blinding din.
      He didn't move; the digging still went on;
Men stooped and shovelled; someone gave a grunt,
                     sludge.
And moaned and died with agony in the (sand:)
Then the long hiss of shells lifted and stopped.

He stared into the gloom; a rocket curved,
          (fretfully) angrily
And rifles rattled (sharply) on the left
Down by the wood, and there was noise of bombs.
      Then the damned English loomed in scrambling haste
Out of the dark and struggled through the wire,
And there were shouts and curses; someone screamed
And men began to (do) blunder down the trench
Without their rifles. It was time to go:
               some
He grabbed his coat; stood up, gulping (the) bread;
Then clutched his head and fell.
          I found him there
In the gray morning when the place was held.
His face was in the mud; one arm flung out
As when he crumpled up; his sturdy legs
Were bent beneath his trunk; heels to the sky.

                Siegfried Sassoon

Right: *Liquid Fire — one of the
new terrors of world war.*

WHEN I'M AMONG A BLAZE OF LIGHTS . . .

When I'm among a blaze of lights,
With tawdry music and cigars
And women dawdling through delights,
And officers at cocktail bars,—
Sometimes I think of garden nights
And elm trees nodding at the stars.

I dream of a small firelit room
With yellow candles burning straight,
And glowing pictures in the gloom,
And kindly books that hold me late.
Of things like these I love to think
When I can never be alone:
Then someone says, "Another drink?"—
And turns my living heart to stone.

Siegfried Sassoon

"The battery grides and jingles,
Mile succeeds to mile; . . ."

THE REDEEMER

Darkness: the rain sluiced down; the mire was deep;
It was past twelve on a mid-winter night,
When peaceful folk in beds lay snug asleep:
There, with much work to do before the light,
We lugged our clay-sucked boots as best we might
Along the trench; sometimes a bullet sang,
And droning shells burst with a hollow bang;
We were soaked, chilled and wretched, every one.
Darkness: the distant wink of a huge gun.

I turned in the black ditch, loathing the storm;
A rocket fizzed and burned with blanching flare,
And lit the face of what had been a form
Floundering in mirk. He stood before me there;
I say that he was Christ; stiff in the glare,
And leaning forward from his burdening task,
Both arms supporting it; his eyes on mine
Stared from the woeful head that seemed a mask
Of mortal pain in Hell's unholy shine.

No thorny crown, only a woollen cap
He wore—an English soldier, white and strong,
Who loved his time like any simple chap,
Good days of work and sport and homely song;
Now he has learned that nights are very long,
And dawn a watching of the windowed sky.
But to the end, unjudging, he'll endure
Horror and pain, not uncontent to die
That Lancaster on Lune may stand secure.

He faced me, reeling in his weariness,
Shouldering his load of planks, so hard to bear.
I say that he was Christ, who wrought to bless
All groping things with freedom bright as air,
And with His mercy washed and made them fair.
Then the flame sank, and all grew black as pitch,
While we began to struggle along the ditch;
And some one flung his burden in the muck,
Mumbling: "O Christ Almighty, now I'm stuck!"

Siegfried Sassoon

BEFORE THE BATTLE

Music of whispering trees
Hushed by a broad-winged breeze
Where shaken water gleams;
And evening radiance falling
With reedy bird-notes calling.
O bear me safe through dark, you low-voiced streams.

I have no need to pray
That fear may pass away;
I scorn the growl and rumble of the fight
That summons me from cool
Silence of marsh and pool
And yellow lilies islanded in light.
O river of stars and shadows, lead me through the night.

Siegfried Sassoon

THE DANCERS
(During a Great Battle, (1916)

The floors are slippery with blood:
The world gyrates too. God is good
That while His wind blows out the light
For those who hourly die for us—
We still can dance, each night.

The music has grown numb with death—
But we will suck their dying breath,
The whispered name they breathed to chance,
To swell our music, make it loud
That we may dance,—may dance.

We are the dull blind carrion-fly
That dance and batten. Though God die
Mad from the horror of the light—
The light is mad, too, flecked with blood,—
We dance, we dance, each night.

Edith Sitwell

BROTHERS

What regiment d'you belong to
brothers?

Word shaking
in the night

Leaf barely born

In the simmering air
involuntary revolt
of the man present at his
brittleness

Brothers

Giuseppe Ungaretti
Trans. Jonathan Griffin

Right: *The Long and the Short of It*
Up Last Draft: *"I suppose you 'as to be careful 'ow
you looks over the parapet about 'ere."*
Out Since Mons: *"You needn't worry, me lad; the
rats are going to be your only trouble."*

1917

"Let it be your pride, therefore, to show all men everywhere not only what good soldiers you are, but also what good men you are. . . Let us set for ourselves a standard so high that it will be a glory to live up to it, and add a new laurel to the crown of America."

President Woodrow Wilson, address to the soldiers of the National Army, April 1917

"Since nations counted money no more than pebbles on a beach, and all would probably repudiate in one form or another at the end of the war, there seemed no reason for stopping, especially as so many people were growing rich by the war; the ladies liked being without their husbands, and all dreaded the settlement afterwards, industrial, political, financial and domestic."

Comment by Colonel Charles à Court Repington, military correspondent of The Times, **visiting France during Third Battle of Ypres (Passchendaele), October 1917**

The year 1917 was the nadir of the war for both sides. Talk of peace died down in both camps, as the German High Command took effective control of Germany and the British and French prepared to launch further offensives. The year, however, saw two major events that were to have incalculable consequences—the Russian Revolution, in which the centuries-old Romanov dynasty was overthrown and the entry of the U.S.A. into the war on the side of the Allies.

War-weariness was affecting both sides, but nowhere was it more pronounced than in Russia, where, in the winter of 1916–17, the war effort more or less collapsed. In February 1917, famine in Petrograd, the Russian capital, and the subsequent unrest sparked off the Russian Revolution. During the course of the year, it became clear that Russia was a spent force—the disintegration of the Eastern Front culminated in the Bolshevik Revolution of October and the subsequent opening of peace negotiations with Germany.

At the same time that one of Germany's enemies was effectively removed from the world stage, the Germans themselves took a step that was to lead to their ultimate downfall. In January 1917, Germany declared that it was once again embarking on a policy of unrestricted submarine warfare. This meant that a clash with the U.S.A. was now inevitable, but the German High Command calculated that Britain could be starved into submission before U.S. intervention could become

Swooping from the West – once drawn into the war the
U.S.A. assisted in the patrolling of the Atlantic.

effective. In response, President Woodrow Wilson broke off diplo-
matic relations with Germany, and in April the U.S.A. declared war.

Even though the entry of the U.S.A. into the war meant that the
industrial might of the New World could now be fully mobilized on the
side of the Allies, the U.S. military presence took time to materialize. In
Britain, relations between Lloyd George, the new Prime Minister, and
Haig, still set on a massive war-winning offensive on the Western Front
despite the carnage of the Somme the previous year, were not good.
Lloyd George failed to persuade his stubborn generals to divert forces to
the Italian and Balkan fronts in an attempt to break the deadlock—only
after the catastrophic Italian defeat at Caporetto late in the year were

WILLS'S CIGARETTES.

GENERAL NIVELLE.

troops rushed to Italy to bolster up the faltering Italian army. In the French camp, despite the misgivings of Pétain, a new Commander-in-Chief, Robert Nivelle, planned his own attempt to win a decisive victory in Champagne. In the event, 1917 saw both plans carried out, but neither achieved the hoped-for victory. The total failure of the Nivelle offensive led to mass mutinies within the French armies, while the massive blows Haig launched in Flanders cost the British equally dear.

LIFE BEHIND THE LINES

1917 opened with a pleasant change for Isaac Rosenberg who was serving in the 11th King's Own Lancasters, part of the 40th Division, some way behind the lines. Exhausted by the endless training marches and soaked in the frozen waters which flooded the trenches, he was moved to the Works Battalion which, he thought, would be much better for his health. Like his fellow soldiers, he was tormented by lice which seemed to survive all manner of disinfectant and de-lousing procedures. *Louse Hunting*, written at this time, immortalizes the curious scene of a group of Tommies, naked as the day they were born, shouting gleefully as their clothes are burned and a whole generation of lice are immolated.

"Nudes—stark and glistening,
Yelling in lurid glee. Grinning faces
And raging limbs
Whirl over the floor one fire.
For a shirt verminously busy
Yon soldier tore from his throat, with oaths
Godhead might shrink at, but not the lice.
And soon the shirt was aflare
Over the candle he'd lit while we lay.

Then we all sprang up and stript
To hunt the verminous brood.
Soon like a demons' pantomime
The place was raging.
See the silhouettes agape,
See the gibbering shadows
Mixed with the battled arms on the wall.
See gargantuan hooked fingers
Pluck in supreme flesh
To smutch supreme littleness.
See the merry limbs in hot Highland fling
Because some wizard vermin
Charmed from the quiet this revel
When our ears were half lulled
By the dark music
Blown from Sleep's trumpet."

An attack! A wiring party going forward.

The manual work he was now engaged in seemed to encourage his imagination, for this was a productive period of writing. When he was assigned to a Field Company of the Royal Engineers one of his duties was to assist in the unloading of barbed wire at night where it was needed on the front lines. Sometimes the limbers rolled over soldiers' corpses lying in No Man's Land. The result of these nightmarish experiences is seen in *Dead Man's Dump*:

"The plunging limbers over the shattered track
Racketed with their rusty freight,
Stuck out like many crowns of thorns,
And the rusty stakes like sceptres old
To stay the flood of brutish men
Upon our brothers dear.

The wheels lurched over sprawled dead
But pained them not, though their bones crunched,
Their shut mouths made no moan.
They lie there huddled, friend and foeman,
Man born of man, and born of woman,
And shells go crying over them
From night till night and now.

Earth has waited for them,
All the time of their growth
Fretting for their decay:
Now she has them at last!
In the strength of their strength
Suspended—stopped and held.

What fierce imaginings their dark souls lit?
Earth! have they gone into you!
Somewhere they must have gone,
And flung on your hard back
Is their soul's sack
Emptied of God-ancestralled essences.
Who hurled them out? Who hurled?

None saw their spirits' shadow shake the grass,
Or stood aside for the half used life to pass
Out of those doomed nostrils and the doomed mouth,
When the swift iron burning bee
Drained the wild honey of their youth.
What of us who, flung on the shrieking pyre,
Walk, our usual thoughts untouched,
Our lucky limbs as on ichor fed,
Immortal seeming ever?
Perhaps when the flames beat loud on us,
A fear may choke in our veins
And the startled blood may stop.

The air is loud with death,
The dark air spurts with fire,
The explosions ceaseless are.
Timelessly now, some minutes past,
These dead strode time with vigorous life,
Till the shrapnel called "An end!"
But not to all. In bleeding pangs
Some borne on stretchers dreamed of home,
Dear things, war-blotted from their hearts.

Maniac Earth! howling and flying, your bowel
Seared by the jagged fire, the iron love,
The impetuous storm of savage love.
Dark Earth! dark Heavens! swinging in chemic smoke,
What dead are born when you kiss each soundless soul
With lightning and thunder from your mined heart,
Which man's self dug, and his blind fingers loosed?

A man's brains splattered on
A stretcher-bearer's face;
His shook shoulders slipped their load,
But when they bent to look again
The drowning soul was sunk too deep
For human tenderness.

They left this dead with the older dead,
Stretched at the cross roads.

Burnt black by strange decay
Their sinister faces lie,
The lid over each eye,
The grass and coloured clay
More motion have than they,
Joined to the great sunk silences.

Here is one not long dead;
His dark hearing caught our far wheels,
And the choked soul stretched weak hands
To reach the living word the far wheels said,
The blood-dazed intelligence beating for light,
Crying through the suspense of the far torturing wheels
Swift for the end to break
Or the wheels to break,
Cried as the tide of the world broke over his sight.

Will they come? Will they ever come?
Even as the mixed hoofs of the mules,
The quivering-bellied mules,
And the rushing wheels all mixed
With his tortured upturned sight.
So we crashed round the bend,
We heard his weak scream,
We heard his very last sound,
And our wheels grazed his dead face."

This poem is now recognized as one of the undoubted masterpieces of First World War poetry, though when Rosenberg sent it to Edward Marsh on 8th May 1917 he confessed he did not think that highly of it.

During this time Rosenberg also wrote several dramatic fragments and completed *Daughters of War*, a poem he had been working on for about a year. On 3rd June he sent a copy to Marsh, who liked it but found it obscure. It was to become Rosenberg's favourite among his own poems, a clear assertion of his belief in the feminine principle.

"THE CRUELLEST MONTH"

During the first six months of the year, therefore, Rosenberg was not involved in active fighting. He was not in the front line of the British attack around Arras at which two other poets—Edward Thomas and Robert Vernède—were killed on 9th April. Edward Thomas died in the blast of a shell. His work will be his own memorial, but Walter de la Mare commemorated him in *To E.T.: 1917*.

When he was killed, Vernède had only recently returned to active service in the Rifle Brigade after recovering from a wound. He had refused to allow a friend in the War Office find him temporary work there where he would be safe. On Easter Day 1917 he wrote to his wife and spoke of the summer at last showing signs of coming on and expressing his hope that the war would end this year. The next morning, 9th April, he was leading his platoon in an attack on Havrincourt Wood; he was in front with a couple of his men when they came upon a concealed German machine gun post. Vernède was hit immediately and, although his men carried him back to the Aid Station, he died. He was buried at the French cemetery at Lechelle. He had been at school with G.K. Chesterton, who remained a lifelong friend. On hearing the news of his death, Chesterton wrote in a letter:

"He always remained, even in face and figure, almost startlingly young. There went with this the paradox of a considerable maturity of mind, even in boyhood. A maturity so tranquil and, as it were, so solitary as to be the very opposite of priggishness. He had a curious intellectual independence . . . He had in everything, even in his very appearance, something that can only be called distinction; something that might be called, in the finer sense, race. This was perhaps the only thing about him, except his name and his critical temper, that suggested something French . . . No man could look more lazy and no man was more active. He would move as swiftly as a leopard from something like sleep to something too unexpected

". . . a sad land, weak with sweats of dearth,
Grey, cratered like the moon with hollow woe,
And pitted with great pocks and scabs of plagues . . ."

*Wilson as the legendary hero, Lohengrin,
coming to France's rescue.*

*to be called gymnastics. It was so that he passed from the English country
life he loved so much, with its gardening and dreaming, to an ambush and
a German gun."*

There are signs that when Vernède was slain he was developing into a
much sharper, more perceptive poet, with a more universal pity. The
shrill and shallow patriotism of his early poetry had evaporated. In *A
Listening Post*, one of the last poems he wrote, there are signs that, had he
lived, he might have developed into a far more questioning poet:

> "The sun's a red ball in the oak
>   And all the grass is grey with dew,
> Awhile ago a blackbird spoke—
>   He didn't know the world's askew.
>
> And yonder rifleman and I
>   Wait here behind the misty trees
> To shoot the first man that goes by,
>   Our rifles ready on our knees.

How could he know that if we fail
  The world may lie in chains for years
And England be a bygone tale
  And right be wrong, and laughter tears?

Strange that this bird sits there and sings
  While we must only sit and plan—
Who are so much the higher things—
  The murder of our fellow man . . .

But maybe God will cause to be—
  Who brought forth sweetness from the strong—
Out of our discords harmony
  Sweeter than that bird's song.''

"Northward incessantly, the flickering gunnery rumbles,
  Far off, like a dull rumour of some other war.
    What are we doing here? . . ."

*"Hers the conflict, hers the conquest, hers the flag
of life unfurled.
Hers the sorrow, hers the suffering, hers the love that
rules the world . . ."*

THE BATTLE OF CHAMPAGNE

The Battle of Arras, at which Thomas and Vernède died, was launched
by the British to support the major French offensive in Champagne, the
Battle of Champagne being Nivelle's plan for a major victory on the
Western Front. Lloyd George, having more confidence in Nivelle than
in Haig, had decided to support the French commander's campaign,
though it was agreed it would be abandoned in favour of Haig's Ypres
offensive should it fail. It was to be a two-handed action on both sides of
the woodlands where the offensive of 1916 had failed. It might have had a
better chance of succeeding if the Germans had not known nearly as
much about it as the Allied commanders: it was openly discussed in
French newspapers, and a detailed Order of Battle was circulated on the
Front—a copy of which got into enemy hands when a French officer was
captured by the Germans. Amply warned, the Germans were able to
keep a watch on the French build-up using air reconnaissance, and the

German command decided to withdraw to a much more highly organized defensive zone, 20 miles behind the line from Arras to Soissons. In the battle the first German line was taken, but otherwise there was no advance and the French suffered heavy casualties. There was a terrible sense of failure, and a loss of confidence in Nivelle who had promised so much. The French army corps mutinied and, to try to control them, several hundred mutineers were shot. All news of the mutinies, however, was suppressed, and Nivelle was replaced by Pétain.

WILLS'S CIGARETTES.

GENERAL PÉTAIN.

THIRD YPRES

The British offensive which followed soon after the Nivelle fiasco distracted German attention from the fact that the French armies were, for the time, a spent force. Haig now brought pressure to bear on those in authority to be allowed to carry out his Ypres campaign. With the ultimate aim of breaking out coastwards to threaten the Belgian ports Germany was using for its submarine campaign, his immediate objective was to secure the right of the Ypres Salient.

Haig wanted to achieve his big victory at Ypres before the rains came. He insisted that his plan, when accomplished, would conclude with the capture of the entire Flemish coast. Such a promise had its attractions, for Admiral Jellicoe believed that through lack of shipping Britain would not be able to continue the war after 1918 unless the Channel ports were recaptured, but Haig still faced considerable opposition from many politicians. Lloyd George feared losses on the same scale as the Somme in 1916, and the nation was already being ransacked to provide civilian manpower for production of armaments as well as troops. The public were war-weary and beginning to grow resentful, but finally Haig got the go-ahead.

Before this major assault, however, on 7th June, General Plumer launched the Battle of Messines which was an unexpected success. The Germans counterattacked to no avail, the British soldiers now occupied the ridge from which they had been slaughtered since the beginning of the war. It was a great boost for British morale, and for the Germans it was demoralizing, as Hindenburg recorded in his memoirs:

"The moral effect of the explosions was simply staggering . . . The 7th June cost us dear . . . it was many days before the front was again secure. The British army did not press its advantage; apparently it only intended to improve its position for the launching of the great Flanders offensive."

Then followed the Third Battle of Ypres, or Passchendaele as it is also known, a name which has become synonymous with military slaughter. The offensive began, as it had at Messines, with a bombardment of shells—four and a half million of them—lasting ten days. Under this barrage the drainage system collapsed and when heavy rains came a sea of mud was the result. It was a terrible instance of military incompetence, for it was clear in advance that the bombardment would destroy the Belgian drainage system, and meteorologists had warned that there would be unusually high levels of rainfall. Also, the Allies knew that the Germans were expecting a major offensive, and Haig's conviction that the enemy would run out of troops flew in the face of intelligence reports. After a promising opening for the Allies on 31st July, the advance failed to make much headway as the Germans had arranged an effective flexible defence system. The attacks, and counter-attacks, continued into early November, with the Germans using mustard gas and the British troops being strafed by enemy aircraft. Passchendaele Ridge and Passchendaele village finally fell to the British by 6th November, but all that had been achieved was the extension of the Salient by about five miles at the cost of 300,000 British, 8,528 French and 260,000 German lives.

Once again the Allies had not won a decisive victory, and only the success at the Battle of Cambrai at the end of November momentarily lifted the Allies' spirits in 1917. The bells of London pealed in celebration, but their joy was desperate, as John Terraine comments:

> "for the time being those bells, with their premature raptures, constituted the most vivid symbol of the frustrated hopes and miserable deceits of 1917. The war's last Christmas approached in unrelieved gloom."

Thus the year ended. German and Russian delegates signed an armistice at Brest-Litovsk on 5th December, and peace negotiations began on 21st December. On 7th December, the U.S.A. declared war on Austria-Hungary. The mood of disillusionment is well presented in the grisly story of a British battalion marching towards action at Ypres who pass a yard where Belgian workmen are engaged in making hundreds of wooden crosses. A soldier shouted out: "Thank 'aig for his vote of confidence!".

SURVIVING THE HOLOCAUST

For one reason or another, Rosenberg was not involved in these major battles of 1917, and thus he luckily avoided the heavy fighting of this period. In September he was granted home leave, but had been so unsettled by the war that relaxation among family and friends was not easy. When he returned to Flanders, British casualties were mounting in the attempt to break out of the Ypres Salient. The weather was terrible with the heavy rains, and Rosenberg fell ill. He was hospitalized, suffering from influenza, until the middle of December, and he had to learn the news of the Ypres offensive and the Battle of Cambrai from other casualties. Late in December he was pronounced fit and sent back to the trenches.

1917 was a year of both action and hospitalization for Ivor Gurney. In January he was training with the 2nd and 5th Gloucestershire

*"And each day one died or another
died: each week we sent out thousands
that returned by hundreds
wounded or gassed . . ."*

Regiment at Varennes (between Albert and Doullens), and in February he was moved to the Ablaincourt sector. Following the German strategic withdrawal, the unit was moved from St. Quentin to Caulincourt, near Vermand. On Good Friday, 6th April, he was wounded in the arm and hospitalized at Rouen for six weeks. In May he was back with his regiment, but transferred to machine-gunnery, and then sent on to the Arras front. At this time he composed some of his finest songs, and in July Sidgwick and Jackson agreed to publish his poems, *Severn and Somme*. When the Ypres offensive began on 31st July the Gloucesters were moved up to the Front. In September, he was gassed at St. Julien, near Passchendaele. He was sent to Bangour War Hospital, near Edinburgh, where he met and fell in love with one of his nurses, Annie Drummond, to whom several of his later poems are dedicated. *Severn and Somme* had some very favourable reviews and a month after its publication he was sent to a signalling course in Northumberland. In his imagination he had never really left the English landscape. In a letter he wrote in the spring of 1917 he said:

"O for a garden to dig in, and music and books in a house of one's own, set in a little valley from whose ridges one may see the Malverns and the Welsh Hills, the plain of Severn and the Severn Sea; to know oneself free

there from the drill-sergeant and the pack, and to order one's life years ahead—plans, doubtless to be broken, but sweet secure plans taking no account of fear or even Prudence but only Joy. One could grow whole and happy there, the mind would lose its sickness and grow strong; it is not possible that health should wait long from such steady and gently beautiful ways of life. The winter's hardships should steel one, the spring bring Joy, summer should perfect this Joy, and autumn bring increase and mellowness to all things, and set the seal of age and ease on things not before secure. I grow happy writing of it."

From the period of his service in 1917, one poem in particular is strikingly original—*The Silent One*—which probably recounts Gurney's personal experience on being told to advance through No Man's Land and finding that, by concentrating his mind on music, he is able to bear up in the midst of death and destruction. Music occupied his mind almost constantly. *Bach and the Sentry* recounts his experiences on sentry-go pondering his beloved Bach preludes. He wonders whether, when he returns to civilian life and plays Bach again, the music will be forever associated with No Man's Land and military duties:

"Watching the dark my spirit rose in flood
  On that most dearest Prelude of my delight.
The low-lying mist lifted its hood,
  The October stars showed nobly in clear night.

When I return, and to real music-making,
  And play that Prelude, how will it happen then?
Shall I feel as I felt, a sentry hardly waking,
  With a dull sense of No Man's Land again."

In view of Gurney's later mental history, this is a deeply prophetic poem as it describes the possibility of a mind completely possessed by the experience of war. As well as music, Gurney turned for comfort to thoughts of his beloved home county Gloucestershire, as did fellow Gloucestershireman F.W. Harvey. Harvey was taken prisoner on the Western Front in 1916 but he continued to write poetry and send it to England from the prisoner-of-war camp. It was published in journals, to much acclaim, and again later in volume form (*Gloucestershire Friends, Comrades in Captivity*).

Harvey's poem *Prisoners* is a lament on behalf of all his comrades for the life of the P.O.W. which removes men from action and the very current of life:

"Comrades of risk and rigour long ago
Who have done battle under honour's name,
Hoped (living or shot down) some need of fame,
And wooed bright Danger for a thrilling kiss,—
Laugh, oh laugh well, that we have come to this!
Laugh, oh laugh loud, all ye who long ago
Adventure found in gallant company!
Safe in Stagnation, laugh, laugh bitterly,
While on this filthiest backwater of Time's flow
Drift we and rot, till something set us free!

Laugh like old men with senses atrophied,
Heeding no Present, to the Future dead,
Nodding quite foolish by the warm fireside
And seeing no flame, but only in the red
And flickering embers, pictures of the past:—
Life like a cinder fading black at last.''

Ford Madox Ford, like Gurney, was gassed at Passchendaele. He was born in Surrey, the son of Dr. Francis Heffer, a German, who was at one time music critic of *The Times*. The poet's grandfather was the painter Ford Madox Brown, and he was connected by marriage to William Rossetti. He changed his name to Ford and after publishing *Poems for Pictures* in 1897 collaborated on two novels with Joseph Conrad. He founded the *English Review* in 1908, and also wrote the trilogy *The Fifth Queen*. After leaving his first wife and refusing to pay her an allowance he served a brief sentence in Brixton prison. He then joined the infantry in Flanders. He is chiefly remembered now for his series of war novels which began in 1915 with the publication of *The Good Soldier*, and continued after the war in a series of linked novels which detail the career of Christopher Tietjens. These novels have been very influential in fashioning our collective perceptions of the war.

"When you saw a Hun sideways he looked something: a serious proposition. Full of ferocity. A Hun up against a Tommy looked like a Holbein landsknecht fighting a music-hall turn. It made you feel that you were indeed a rag-time army. Rubbed it in.''

(No More Parades)

His extensive poem *Antwerp* contains the following description of Charing Cross station as the wounded are brought in from Flanders:

David Lloyd George.

"This is Charing Cross;
It is midnight;
There is a great crowd
And no light.
A great crowd, all black that hardly whispers aloud.
Surely, that is a dead woman—a dead mother!
She has a dead face;
She is dressed all in black;
She wanders to the bookstall and back,
At the back of the crowd;
And back again and again back,
She sways and wanders.

This is Charing Cross;
It is one o'clock.
There is still a great cloud, and very little light;
Immense shafts of shadows over the black crowd
That hardly whispers aloud . . .
And now! . . . That is another dead mother,
And there is another and another and another . . .
And little children, all in black,
All with dead faces, waiting in all the waiting-places,
Wandering from the doors of the waiting-room
In the dim gloom.

These are the women of Flanders.
They await the lost.
They await the lost that shall never leave the dock;
They await the lost that shall never again come by the train
To the embraces of all these women with dead faces;
They await the lost who lie dead in trench and barrier and foss,
In the dark of the night.
This is Charing Cross; it is past one of the clock;
There is very little light.

There is so much pain."

LATENT PROTEST AND GROWING CYNICISM

Robert Graves and Siegfried Sassoon had both agreed by the opening of 1917 that the war was deplorable but that they should make no public protest. Their task, they believed, was to show that poets were men of courage and consequently they returned to the Front. The year was to be momentous for them both. In January, Graves was posted as an instructor to Harfleur—the base where newly arrived troops were trained. He was not happy there, but was back in the trenches on the Somme by early February. Captain J.C. Dunn, R.A.M.C., considered

Graves to be unfit, as indeed proved to be the case. He fell ill during the cold weather, and his bronchitis was severely aggravated by the poor condition of his lungs that had barely recovered from when he was wounded the previous July. He was sent to hospital at Rouen and his active service was brought to an end. He was sent to Somerville College, Oxford, which had been turned into a hospital, and then, when he had recovered, he served the Wadham Company of the University Officer Training Corps as an instructor. But even this proved too much for him: he collapsed and fell down a staircase, and was dispatched to Somerville again, and then to convalesce on the Isle of Wight.

Sassoon, meanwhile, was serving heroically in the 2nd Battalion of the Royal Welch Fusiliers, but the poetry he wrote at this stage clearly shows his disillusionment:

> "If I were fierce, and bald, and short of breath,
>   I'd live with scarlet Majors at the Base,
> And speed glum heroes up the line to death.
>   You'd see me with my puffy petulant face,
> Guzzling and gulping in the best hotel,
>   Reading the Roll of Honour. "Poor young chap,"
> I'd say—"I used to know his father well;
>   Yes, we've lost heavily in this last scrap."
> And when the war is done and youth stone dead,
>   I'd toddle safely home and die—in bed.''

(*Base Details*)

He took part in the offensive that opened on 9th April at Arras. The poem *Trench Duty* captures the essence of trench warfare:

> "Shaken from sleep, and numbed and scarce awake,
> Out in the trench with three hours' watch to take,
> I blunder through the splashing mirk; and then
> Hear the gruff muttering voices of the men
> Crouching in cabins candle-chinked with light.
> Hark! There's the big bombardment on our right
> Rumbling and bumping; and the dark's a glare
> Of flickering horror in the sectors where
> We raid the Boche; men waiting, stiff and chilled,
> Or crawling on their bellies through the wire.
> 'What? Stretcher-bearers wanted? Someone killed?'
> Five minutes ago I heard a sniper fire:
> Why did he do it? . . . Starlight overhead—
> Blank stars. I'm wide-awake; and some chap's dead."

The entries in his diary during April 1917 catalogue the moods, physical privations and horrors of these days as they pass:

"Writing this in a tiny dug-out, but luckily it has a stove . . . Rations getting very short. Only one meal today, and that scrappy to a degree . . . A fair amount of gun-rumbling going on all round . . . Up to the neck in war this time, anyhow. Quite impossible to sleep as it is bitter cold and nowhere to lie down. (April 12th) Remained in the same trench. Weather fine. 62nd Division attacked in front this morning—from a hill about three-quarters of a mile away. Objective was a village called Fontaine-les-Croisilles—and the wood, Fontaine Wood. Attack failed owing to the left flank being unsupported . . . A good many dead lying in front of our trench. Our troops are a little way down the far slope: on the left they are still in the Hindenburg Line, above the village and River Sensée. Our Brigade attacks the same place tomorrow at 5.30. We are in reserve. We are astride the Hindenburg Line on the hill. (April 13th)"

These experiences Sassoon worked into poetry, distilling what he had seen and felt and heard. For example, *The Rear-Guard (Hindenburg Line, April 1917)*.

It is impossible not to be impressed with the very wide range of Sassoon's war poetry. It encompasses an extensive variety of subject matter and explores many moods—horrific, satiric, elegiac and comic. Poems such as *Counter-Attack* preserve the terrors and insanity of modern war in the aspic of genius:

> "We'd gained our first objective hours before
> While dawn broke like a face with blinking eyes,
> Pallid, unshaved and thirsty, blind with smoke.
> Things seemed all right at first. We held their line,
> With bombers posted, Lewis guns well placed,
> And clink of shovels deepening the shallow trench.
> The place was rotten with dead; green clumsy legs
> High-booted, sprawled and grovelled along the saps;
> And trunks, face downward in the sucking mud,
> Wallowed like trodden sand-bags loosely filled;
> And naked sodden buttocks, mats of hair,
> Bulged, clotted heads, slept in the plastering slime.
> And then the rain began,—the jolly old rain!
>
> A yawning soldier knelt against the bank,
> Staring across the morning blear with fog;
> He wondered when the Allemands would get busy;
> And then, of course, they started with five-nines
> Traversing, sure as fate, and never a dud.
> Mute in the clamour of shells he watched them burst
> Spouting dark earth and wire with gusts from hell,
> While posturing giants dissolved in drifts of smoke.
> He crouched and flinched, dizzy with galloping fear,
> Sick for escape,—loathing the strangled horror
> And butchered, frantic gestures of the dead.

An officer came blundering down the trench:
"Stand-to and man the fire-step!" On he went . . .
Gasping and bawling, "Fire-step . . . counter-attack!"
Then the haze lifted. Bombing on the right
Down the old sap: machine-guns on the left;
And stumbling figures looming out in front.
"O Christ, they're coming at us!" Bullets spat,
And he remembered his rifle . . . rapid fire . . .
And started blazing wildly . . . then a bang
Crumpled and spun him sideways, knocked him out
To grunt and wriggle: none heeded him; he choked
And fought the flapping veils of smothering gloom,
Lost in a blurred confusion of yells and groans . . .
Down, and down, and down, he sank and drowned,
Bleeding to death. The counter-attack had failed."

The horrors of the war are immediately transformed by his imagination into outbursts of powerful poetry. On 22nd April 1917, he saw a heap of earth thrown up by a big shell explosion. Sticking out of the muddy soil two hands stuck out: "like the roots of a shrub turned upside down. They might have been imploring aid; they might have been groping and struggling for life and release". The same day he wrote *To the Warmongers*:

"I'm back again from hell
With loathsome thoughts to sell;
Secrets of death to tell;
And horrors from the abyss.

Young faces bleared with blood,
Sucked down into the mud,
You shall hear things like this,
Till the tormented slain

Crawl round and once again,
With limbs that twist awry
Moan out their brutish pain,
As the fighters pass them by.

For you our battles shine
With triumph half-divine;
And the glory of the dead
Kindles in each proud eye.

But a curse is on my head,
That shall not be unsaid,
And the wounds in my heart are red,
For I have watched them die."

Latent in this poem is the protest which he was to voice fully in July 1917.

Sassoon was wounded by a sniper's bullet through the shoulder during the attack on Fontaine-les-Croisilles. In his diary he notes that, in the circumstances of war, death dominates all perceptions:

"stumbling along the trench in the dusk, dead men and living lying against the sides of the trenches—one never knew which were dead and which living. Dead and living were very nearly one, for death was in all our hearts."

(17th April 1917)

All round him the conversation of his wounded fellows is of the war. *Does it Matter?* shows another, more cynical, side to the theme of the wounded in hospital:

"Does it matter?—losing your legs? . . .
For people will always be kind,
And you need not show that you mind
When the others come in after hunting
To gobble their muffins and eggs.

Does it matter?—losing your sight? . . .
There's such splendid work for the blind;
And people will always be kind,
As you sit on the terrace remembering
And turning your face to the light.

Do they matter?—those dreams from the pit? . . .
You can drink and forget and be glad,
And people won't say that you're mad;
For they'll know that you've fought for your country,
And no one will worry a bit."

ENGLAND, A CHANGED LAND

Sassoon was sent home to England to recover, but the country to which he returned was very different to the one he had known before the war. German submarine warfare was taking a terrible toll of British merchant shipping. In 1917, 2,000,000 tons of shipping had been sunk, and at times the country's food stocks were reduced to a level sufficient only to last four weeks. In February, "war bread" had been introduced that was made from flour milled at an extraction rate of 81 per cent, and had a compulsory admixture of 5 per cent barley, oat or rye flour to stretch supplies. Lord Devonport, the Food Controller, put strict limits on bread and sugar consumption. It was feared that rising prices and poor distribution might lead to industrial unrest, but in fact the war had brought full employment and the general standard of living in the

A German view of death, in the form of the
U-boat blockade, threatening England.

industrial working classes improved on its pre-war standard. British military conscription revealed that only three out of nine conscripts of military age were actually fit for service as a result of malnutrition. If you could afford it, social life in the bigger cities was still attractive and restaurants did a thriving trade.

Meanwhile the impact of the war was changing the social role of women for ever. Those employed in munitions cut their hair short as a safety measure and bobbed hair became all the rage. Smoking, too, became acceptable. In July 1915, tens of thousands of women and 90 bands had paraded in London demanding war work. The procession was led by the formidable Mrs. Pankhurst. At that time there were only 50,000 women in munitions factories, while Germany employed 500,000. By 1917, however, women were to be found not only in munitions, but in engineering, shipyards and factories, as well as in clerical and administrative employment.

A PACIFIST IS BORN

While convalescing Sassoon enjoyed the company of Robert ("Robbie") Ross, man of letters and patron of aspiring artists, chiefly remembered for his loyal friendship with Oscar Wilde, Edmund Gosse, H.G. Wells, Arnold Bennett, and the poet and journalist J.C. Squire. Sassoon described Squire as a:

"vegetarian—sad-looking type of poetical person with hair rather long brushed tidily over right eyebrow. Slouching gait, hands in pockets . . . Looks more like an actor."

Squire was rather taken aback by the strong pacifist sentiments which were now developing in Sassoon. As Gurney had turned to music to help keep a sense of order in his existence during active service, so Sassoon drew on literature. He read *Far From the Madding Crowd* in the trenches, and constantly read and re-read the Metaphysical poets. He memorized Keats. His collection of poems, *The Old Huntsman*, was published on 8th May and was well reviewed. Among the congratulatory letters he had was one from Thomas Hardy who was very pleased with the book. "The general spirit, choice of subject, energy, and 'don't care-a-damness', and youthfulness give me deep satisfaction", was Arnold Bennett's comment. Virginia Woolf, in *The Times Literary Supplement*, praised it:

"What Mr. Sassoon has felt to be the most sordid and horrible experiences in the world he makes us feel to be so in a measure which no other poet of the war has achieved. As these jaunty matter-of-fact statements succeed each other, such loathing, such hatred accumulates behind them that we say to ourselves: 'Yes, this is going on; and we are sitting here watching it,' with a new shock of surprise, with an uneasy desire to leave our place in the audience, which is a tribute to Mr. Sassoon's power as a realist. It is realism of the right, of the poetic kind."

The pig replaces the pug – rigours
of war on the home front.

A POET'S DISSENT

In the summer of 1917 Sassoon decided that he would have to manifest his disapproval of the war. He believed that the war could and should be brought to an end by an armistice between the Allies and the Central Powers, for both sides must now have realized that nothing was to be gained from prolonging the conflict and as, he thought, neither side could win outright only further insufferable sacrifices of human lives could result.

On 6th July 1917, Siegfried Sassoon sent his Commanding Officer the following statement:

> "I am making this statement as an act of wilful defiance of military authority, because I believe that the War is being deliberately prolonged by those who have the power to end it. I am a soldier, convinced that I am acting on behalf of soldiers. I believe that this War, on which I entered as a war of defence and liberation, has now become a war of aggression and conquest. I believe that the purpose for which I and my fellow soldiers entered upon this war should have been so clearly stated as to have made it impossible to change them, and that, had this been done, the objects which actuated us would now be attainable by negotiation. I have seen and endured the sufferings of the troops, and I can no longer be a party to prolong these sufferings for ends which I believe to be evil and unjust. I am not protesting against the conduct of the war, but against the political errors and insincerities for which the fighting men are being sacrificed. On behalf of those who are suffering now I make this protest against the deception which is being practised on them; also I believe that I may help to destroy the callous complacency with which the majority of those at home regard the contrivance of agonies which they do not, and which they have not sufficient imagination to realize."

He sent copies to several leading public figures, including Thomas Hardy, Arnold Bennett, Edward Carpenter, Edward Marsh and H.G. Wells. It was read out in the House of Commons on 30th July and printed in *The Times* on 31st July. Sassoon overstayed his leave by a week and then received a letter from his Adjutant requesting him to rejoin his battalion at Litherland immediately. He then wrote to the Commanding Officer of the 3rd Royal Welch Fusiliers in which he explained that it was his intention to refuse to perform any further military duties, "as a protest against the policy of the government in prolonging the war by failing to state their conditions of peace". He went on to say that he was doing all he could to make things as easy as possible for his C.O. in dealing with his case and that he was fully aware of what he was letting himself in for.

On 12th July, Sassoon reported at Litherland and stayed at Liverpool. He refused to attend a medical board but was eventually persuaded by Robert Graves to attend one on 20th July. Graves knew from personal experience that Sassoon had been pushed beyond the point of endurance. Graves believed his friend was near to madness. Sassoon told him he saw corpses lying round him in the street, that he would like to shoot the Prime Minister and Sir Douglas Haig. He also had an irresistible urge to go back to the Front and get himself killed. In Graves' opinion Bertrand Russell and other pacifists were exploiting Sassoon's emotional condition to further their cause, and that Russell had actually assisted Sassoon in the composition of his statement. (Russell appears as Tyrrell in Sassoon's *Memoirs of an Infantry Officer*.) The statement was published as a pamphlet and circulated and eventually stocks were seized by the police. While Russell was contemplating how best to exploit Sassoon as a military hero-pacifist for the advantage of his Non-Conscription Movement, Graves, posted to Liverpool, tried to persuade Sassoon to give up his protest. The matter would be smoothed over, he said, if Sassoon agreed to attend a medical board. If he insisted on continuing this action he would be certified as insane. At this stage Sassoon hoped for a court martial, as this would give him the publicity he needed to fully capitalize on his protest statement. Graves appeared as a witness for the medical board and the result was that Sassoon became a patient at Craiglockhart War Hospital—for shell-shocked officers—at Slateford, near Edinburgh. Sassoon arrived here on 23rd July. Among his fellow patients was Wilfred Owen.

OWEN ON THE SOMME

Wilfred Owen had had an eventful year. In September 1916 he had applied for a transfer from the infantry to the Royal Flying Corps, had been interviewed in London, but had not been successful. Early in January 1917 he was with the Manchesters on the Somme, near Beaumont Hamel. On 4th January he sent his mother the news:

Two-tier bridges over the swamps of Flanders: cavalry crossing over infantry filing into trenches.

"Since I set foot on Calais I have not had dry feet . . . At the base . . . it was not so bad . . . After those two days we were let down, gently, into the real thing. Mud. It has penetrated now into that Sanctuary my sleeping bag, and that holy of holies my pyjamas. For I sleep on a stone floor and the servant squashed mud on all my belongings; I suppose by way of baptism. We are three officers in this 'Room', the rest of the house is occupied by servants and the band; the roughest set of knaves I have ever been herded with. Even now their vile language is shaking the flimsy door between the rooms."

His privations were to continue and to get worse: everything was makeshift, the rain was freezing, mud was universal. They moved to the Front. Moving about in the trenches involved wading in water with a mean depth of two feet. Shelling was constant. On one occasion he held a dugout in No Man's Land for 50 hours, with 25 men and water up to the depth of two feet: "I nearly broke down and let myself drown in the water that was now slowly rising over my knees", he wrote. One of the sentries was blown down and blinded. This experience is the basis of *The Sentry* which he began at Craiglockhart between August and October 1917 and did not finish until September 1918:

"We'd found an old Boche dug-out, and he knew,
And gave us hell; for shell on frantic shell
Lit full on top, but never quite burst through.
Rain, guttering down in waterfalls of slime,
Kept slush waist-high and rising hour by hour,
And choked the steps too thick with clay to climb.
What murk of air remained stank old, and sour
With fumes from whizbangs, and the smell of men
Who'd lived there years, and left their curse in the den,
If not their corpses . . .
               There we herded from the blast
Of whizbangs; but one found our door at last,—
Buffeting eyes and breath, snuffing the candles,
And thud! flump! thud! down the steep steps thumping
And sploshing in the flood, deluging muck,
The sentry's body; then his rifle, handles
Of old Boche bombs, and mud in ruck on ruck.
We dredged it up, for dead, until he whined
"O sir—my eyes,—I'm blind,—I'm blind, I'm blind."
Coaxing, I held a flame against his lids
And said if he could see the least blurred light
He was not blind; in time they'd get all right.
"I can't," he sobbed. Eyeballs, huge-bulged like squids',
Watch my dreams still,—yet I forgot him there
In posting Next for duty, and sending a scout
To beg a stretcher somewhere, and flound'ring about
To other posts under the shrieking air.

Those other wretches, how they bled and spewed,
And one who would have drowned himself for good,
I try not to remember these things now.
Let Dread hark back for one word only: how,
Half-listening to that sentry's moans and jumps,
And the wild chattering of his shivered teeth,
Renewed most horribly whenever crumps
Pummelled the roof and slogged the air beneath,
Through the dense din, I say, we heard him shout
"I see your lights!"—But ours had long gone out."

In one of his letters to his mother he describes the battlefield as the eternal place of gnashing of teeth, and says that the Slough of Despond could be contained in one of its craters; the fires of Sodom and Gomorrah could not light a candle to it "to find the way to Babylon the fallen". It was pock-marked like a body of foulest disease and its odour was the breath of cancer. This vision marinated in his imagination for months, together with the deep impressions made on him by his reading (later in the year) of Henry Barbusse's classic novel of the Great War, *Le Feu*, and these images can clearly be seen in many of his poems.

Respite came in the form of a course on transport duties at Abbeville in February and when Owen returned at the end of the month, even though there was still snow on the ground, he sensed that spring was near. He joined the battalion again near Fresnoy. One night in mid-March, Owen was groping his way in the darkness to help a man who was in a dangerous state of exhaustion when he fell 15 feet down a well and suffered concussion (it might have been a shell hole in a cellar floor). He was hospitalized and rejoined his battalion at the beginning of April.

GOING "OVER THE TOP"

On 12th April the battalion was in action at Savy Wood, where they were strafed with machine-gun fire and high explosive shells. We have his account of these moments:

"The sensations of going over the top are about as exhilarating as those dreams of falling over a precipice . . . I woke up without being squashed. Some didn't. There was an extraordinary exultation in the act of slowly walking forward, showing ourselves openly.

There was no bugle and no drum for which I am very sorry. I kept up a kind of chanting sing-song: Keep the Line straight! Not so far on the left! Steady on the left! Not so fast!"

When Owen looked back and saw the ground crawling with wounded bodies all he felt was exultation at having survived the barrage unscathed. In fact, although he had physically survived unhurt, damage had been done on a deeper psychological level. The Brigade was relieved

*"They must take part in
defacing and destroying
the natural body . . ."*

on 21st April by the 14th Brigade and moved back to the village of
Quivières. Lieutenant Colonel Luxmoore, Owen's Commanding Officer, noticed that he was showing signs of severe strain. Referred to the
M.O., Owen was found to be suffering from a confused memory and to
be shaky and subject to tremors. This was diagnosed as shell shock and
he was sent to England. After a period in hospital at Netley, Hampshire,
he was sent to Craiglockhart where he responded well to treatment
supervised by the brilliant and humane Dr. W.H.R. Rivers, a pioneer in
the treatment of mental disorder brought on by active service.

TWO POETS MEET

Owen was well established as a patient at Craiglockhart when Sassoon
arrived. Owen was greatly impressed when he read *The Old Huntsman*,
he wrote to his mother on 15th August saying:

"*I have just been reading Siegfried Sassoon, and am feeling at a very high pitch of emotion. Nothing like his trench life sketches has ever been written or ever will be written. Shakespeare reads vapid after these.*"

At first, Owen was unable to pluck up the courage to go and introduce himself, but after a few days he gathered himself up and knocked on Sassoon's door. Sassoon described the scene in *Siegfried's Journey 1916–1920*:

"*Short, dark-haired, and shyly hesitant, he stood for a moment before coming across to the window . . . A favourable first impression was made by the fact that he had under his arm several copies of* The Old Huntsman *. . . He spoke with a slight stammer, which was no unusual thing in that neurosis-pervaded hospital . . . He had a charming honest smile, and his manners . . . were modest and ingratiating.*"

Sassoon autographed the books for Owen's friends and then signed one for Owen himself, unaware at that time that the name Wilfred Owen would become celebrated. Owen and Sassoon talked about poetry—mostly about Sassoon's—and at the end of this conversation Owen confessed that he, too, was a poet, as yet unpublished. Sassoon

"*And when the summons in our ears was shrill
Unshaken in our trust we rose, . . .*"

"O road in dizzy moonlight bleak and blue,
With forlorn effigies of farms besprawled,
With trees bitterly bare or snapped in two, . . ."

wondered how good he was: "He had seemed an interesting little chap but had not struck me as remarkable . . . my first view of him was as a rather ordinary young man, perceptibly provincial".

This was the first of many meetings. During the days Sassoon played golf and Owen went picnicking or seeing the sights; in the evenings the two writers talked about poetry and under Sassoon's creative and constructive criticism, Owen's genius flowered. Owen was the Editor of *The Hydra-Journal of the Craiglockhart War Hospital*, and this took up much of his time, but the first of his poems to be published—*Song of Songs*—appeared in its pages on 1st September 1917. This was a short lyric which Sassoon praised, but Owen soon outgrew it.

Sassoon was impressed by Owen's cheerfulness and modesty. He did not seem prey to emotions, except when thinking about the war. He recorded that Owen's voice was soft and velvety, which somehow suggested "the Keatsian richness of his poetry . . . it had the texture of soft consonants & suggested crimsons & sumptuous browns".

Sassoon's influence on Owen began to show itself in the use of direct speech and colloquialisms and in a general sharpening of focus. At this time Owen wrote *Anthem for Doomed Youth*, and there exists a draft in Owen's handwriting, with his comment at the foot of the page: "With Sassoon's amendments". The title of the poem was actually Sassoon's suggestion.

> "What passing-bells for these who die as cattle?
>   —Only the monstrous anger of the guns.
>   Only the stuttering rifles' rapid rattle
> Can patter out their hasty orisons.
> No mockeries now for them; no prayers nor bells;
>   Nor any voice of mourning save the choirs,—
> The shrill, demented choirs of wailing shells;
>   And bugles calling for them from sad shires.
>
> What candles may be held to speed them all?
>   Not in the hands of boys, but in their eyes
> Shall shine the holy glimmers of goodbyes.
>   The pallor of girls' brows shall be their pall;
> Their flowers the tenderness of patient minds,
> And each slow dusk a drawing-down of blinds."

Robert Graves came to visit Sassoon early in October, and was introduced to Wilfred, who showed him the draft of a new poem, *Disabled*, with which Graves was greatly impressed. Owen, for his part, was struck by the contrast between Graves' physical appearance—"He is a big, rather plain fellow, the last man on earth apparently capable of the extraordinary, delicate fancies of his books"—and his poetry. This

"A man of mine
Lies on the wire.
It is death to fetch his soulless corpse . . ."

was on 13th October. The meeting was an inspiration to Owen, who wrote six poems in the following week. Among them was the rightly celebrated *Dulce et Decorum Est*:

"Bent double, like old beggars under sacks,
Knock-kneed, coughing like hags, we cursed through sludge,
Till on the haunting flares we turned our backs
And towards our distant rest began to trudge.
Men marched asleep. Many had lost their boots
But limped on, blood-shod. All went lame; all blind;
Drunk with fatigue; deaf even to the hoots
Of gas shells dropping softly behind.

Gas! GAS! Quick, boys!—An ecstasy of fumbling,
Fitting the clumsy helmets just in time;
But someone still was yelling out and stumbling,
And flound'ring like a man in fire or lime . . .
Dim, through the misty panes and thick green light,
As under a green sea, I saw him drowning.

In all my dreams, before my helpless sight,
He plunges at me, guttering, choking, drowning.

If in some smothering dreams you too could pace
Behind the wagon that we flung him in,
And watch the white eyes writhing in his face,
His hanging face, like a devil's sick of sin;
If you could hear, at every jolt, the blood
Come gargling from the froth-corrupted lungs,
Obscene as cancer, bitter as the cud
Of vile, incurable sores on innocent tongues,—
My friend, you would not tell with such high zest
To children ardent for some desperate glory,
The old Lie: Dulce et decorum est
Pro patria mori."

RETURN TO THE FRONT

On 28th October Owen appeared before the Medical Board and was granted three weeks' leave pending return to his unit. Sassoon gave him a sealed letter which contained a £10 note and "Robbie" Ross's London address. In London he met Ross at the Reform Club and was introduced to H.G. Wells and Arnold Bennett. Before the end of November he joined the 5th Manchesters at Scarborough. He was promoted lieutenant in early December and went to Craiglockhart to visit friends. Sassoon was passed fit for service at the end of November. He wrote to Robert Graves:

"The Board asked if I had changed my views on the war, and I said I hadn't, which seemed to cause surprise. However Rivers obtained, previously, an assurance from a high quarter that no obstacles would be put in the way of my going back to the sausage machine."

At Christmas he was posted back to France, but he resolved "to lead a life of light-hearted stupidity". He had done all he could to protest against the war and he decided to be as peaceful-minded as he could, as the only way he could hope to survive the horrors of the Front.

Edmund Blunden had been surviving those horrors throughout 1917:

"Beyond the area called Thiepval . . . a trench . . . led forward; unhappy he who got into it! It was blasted out by intense bombardment . . . and pools of mortar-like mud filled most of it. . . The wooden track ended and then the men fought their way on through the gluey morass, until not one or two were reduced to tears and impotent wild cries to God . . . the Schwaben Redoubt ahead was an almost obliterated cocoon of trenches in which mud, and death, and life were much the same thing—and there the deep dugouts . . . were cancerous with torn bodies, and to pass an entrance was to gulp poison . . . Men of the next battalion were found in mud up to the armpits . . . those who found them could not get them out. The whole zone was a corpse, and the mud itself mortified."

This is how he recorded his impressions during the Ypres offensive when he came to write *Undertones of War*. Vlamertinghe, a village west of Ypres, which endured much bombardment, was immortalized by Blunden in *Vlamertinghe: Passing the Chateau, July 1917*:

"'And all her silken flanks with garlands drest'—
But we are coming to the sacrifice.
Must those have flowers who are not yet gone West?
May those have flowers who live with death and lice?
This must be the floweriest place
That earth allows; the queenly face
Of the proud mansion borrows grace for grace
Spite of those brute guns lowing at the skies.

Bold great daisies' golden lights,
Bubbling roses' pinks and whites—
Such a gay carpet! poppies by the million;
Such damask! such vermilion!
But if you ask me, mate, the choice of colour
Is scarcely right; this red should have been duller."

On the night of 19th September, amid pouring rain and thick morning mist, 11 British Divisions advanced on Bassevillebeek, Polygon Wood and Gravenstafel Ridge. The attack was successful and several enemy positions were taken—Inverness Copse, Veldhoek, Polderhoek, Glencorse Wood and Nonne Boschen. The enemy counterattacked strongly in the vicinity of the Menin Road, but by the 26th Polygon Wood was cleared, together with Zonnebeke. The fury of the German response was immediate, and the event is the subject of Blunden's *The Zonnebeke Road*, which will portray forever that moment in the Third Battle of Ypres.

Even during the bleak and terrifying year of 1917, Blunden did not lose touch with the sustaining love of the landscape and its ability to support human life. These feelings are strongly expressed in *Rural Economy*, which dates from this time, even though edged with irony.

"There was winter in those woods
    And still it was July
There were Thule solitudes
    With thousands huddling nigh;
There the fox had left his den,
The scraped holes hid not stoats but men.

To these woods the rumour teemed
    Of peace five miles away;
In sight, hills hovered, houses gleamed
    Where last perhaps we lay
Till the cockerels bawled bright morning and
The hours of life slipped the slack hand.

In sight, life's farms sent forth their gear,
    Here rakes and ploughs lay still,
Yet, save some curious clods, all here
    Was raked and ploughed with a will.
The sower was the ploughman too,
And iron seeds broadcast he threw.

What husbandry could outdo this?
    With flesh and blood he fed
The planted iron that nought amiss
    Grew thick and swift and red,
And in a night though ne'er so cold
Those acres bristled a hundredfold.

Why, even the wood as well as field
    This thoughtful farmer knew
Could be reduced to plough and tilled
    And if he planned, he'd do;
The field and wood, all bone-fed loam,
Shot up a roaring harvest home."

This poem should always be read in conjunction with his more celebrated poem of 1917, *Third Ypres*.

THIRD YPRES

"Triumph! How strange, how strong had triumph come
On weary hate of foul and endless war
When from its grey gravecloths awoke anew
The summer day. Among the tumbled wreck
Of fascined lines and mounds the light was peering,
Half-smiling upon us, and our newfound pride;
The terror of the waiting night outlived,
The time too crowded for the heart to count
All the sharp cost in friends killed on the assault.
No hook of all the octopus had held us,
Here stood we trampling down the ancient tyrant.
So shouting dug we among the monstrous pits.
Amazing quiet fell upon the waste,
Quiet intolerable to those who felt
The hurrying batteries beyond the masking hills
For their new parley setting themselves in array
In crafty forms unmapped.
                              No, these, smiled Faith,
Are dumb for the reason of their overthrow.
They move not back, they lie among the crews
Twisted and choked, they'll never speak again.
Only the copse where once might stand a shrine
Still clacked and suddenly hissed its bullets by.
The War would end, the Line was on the move,
And at a bound the impassable was passed.
We lay and waited with extravagant joy.

Now dulls the day and chills; comes there no word
From those who swept through our new lines to flood
The lines beyond? but little comes, and so
Sure as a runner time himself's accosted.
And the slow moments shake their heavy heads,
And croak, 'They're done, they'll none of them get through.
They're done, they've all died on the entanglements,
The wire stood up like an unplashed hedge and thorned
With giant spikes—and there they've paid the bill.'
Then comes the black assurance, then the sky's
Mute misery lapses into trickling rain,
That wreathes and swims and soon shuts in our world,
And those distorted guns, that lay past use,
Why—miracles not over!—all a-firing!
The rain's no cloak from their sharp eyes. And you,
Poor signaller, you I passed by this emplacement,
You whom I warned, poor daredevil, waving your flags,
Among this screeching I pass you again and shudder
At the lean green flies upon the red flesh madding.

Runner, stand by a second. Your message.—He's gone,
Falls on a knee, and his right hand uplifted
Claws his last message from his ghostly enemy,
Turns stone-like. Well I liked him, that young runner,
But there's no time for that. O now for the word
To order us flash from these drowning roaring traps
And even hurl upon that snarling wire?
Why are our guns so impotent?
                                    The grey rain,
Steady as the sand in an hourglass on this day,
Where through the window the red lilac looks,
And all's so still, the chair's odd click is noise—
The rain is all heaven's answer, and with hearts
Past reckoning we are carried into night
And even sleep is nodding here and there.
The second night steals through the shrouding rain.
We in our numb thought crouching long have lost
The mockery triumph, and in every runner
Have urged the mind's eye see the triumph to come
The sweet relief, the straggling out of hell
Into whatever burrows may be given
For life's recall. Then the fierce destiny speaks.
This was the calm, we shall look back for this.
The hour is come; come, move to the relief!
Dizzy we pass the mule-strewn track where once
The ploughman whistled as he loosed his team;
And where he turned home-hungry on the road,
The leaning pollard marks us hungrier turning.
We crawl to save the remnant who have torn
Back from the tentacled wire, those whom no shell
Has charred into black carcasses—Relief!
They grate their teeth until we take their room,
And through the churn of moonless night and mud
And flaming burst and sour gas we are huddled
Into the ditches where they bawl sense awake,
And in a frenzy that none could reason calm
(Whimpering some, and calling on the dead),
They turn away: as in a dream they find
Strength in their feet to bear back that strange whim
Their body.
         At the noon of the dreadful day
Our trench and death's is on a sudden stormed
With huge and shattering salvoes, the clay dances
In founts of clods around the concrete sties,
Where still the brain devises some last armour
To live out the poor limbs.
                              This wrath's oncoming
Found four of us together in a pillbox,

Skirting the abyss of madness with light phrases,
White and blinking, in false smiles grimacing.
The demon grins to see the game, a moment
Passes, and—still the drum-tap dongs my brain
To a whirring void—through the great breach above me
The light comes in with icy shock and the rain
Horribly drips. Doctor, talk, talk! if dead
Or stunned I know not; the stinking powdered concrete,
The lyddite turns me sick—my hair's all full
Of this smashed concrete. O, I'll drag you, friends,
Out of the sepulchre into the light of day,
For this is day, the pure and sacred day.
And while I squeak and gibber over you,
Look, from the wreck a score of field-mice nimble,
And tame and curious look about them; (these
Calmed me, on these depended my salvation).
There comes my sergeant, and by all the powers
The wire is holding to the right battalion,
And I can speak—but I myself first spoken
Hear a known voice now measured even to madness
Call me by name.
           'For God's sake send and help us,
Here in a gunpit, all headquarters done for,
Forty or more, the nine-inch came right through,
All splashed with arms and legs, and I myself
The only one not killed nor even wounded.
You'll send—God bless you!' The more monstrous fate
Shadows our own, the mind swoons doubly burdened,
Taught how for miles our anguish groans and bleeds,
A whole sweet countryside amuck with murder;
Each moment puffed into a year with death
Still wept the rain, roared guns,
Still swooped into the swamps of flesh and blood,
All to the drabness of uncreation sunk,
And all thought dwindled to a moan, Relieve!
But who with what command can now relieve
The dead men from that chaos, or my soul?''

THE END OF THE YEAR

Blunden's *Third Ypres*, written in November, vividly conveys the feeling of helplessness which many felt by the end of the year as the war dragged on in a seemingly timeless way. It was as if it had a life of its own: "But who with what command can now relieve/ The dead men from that chaos, or my soul?". Despite the U.S.A. having declared war on Germany in April, no U.S. troops actually went into action until late October and they had therefore played only a limited role in the year's battles. However, the U.S. was now mobilized, the men of the New World had come to the aid of the old to shed their blood on the Western Front, and their presence gave hope for 1918. In the twilight of the old year, fresh to the war and to Europe, John Peale Bishop from Virginia wrote *In the Dordogne*:

"We stood up before day
and shaved by metal mirrors
in the faint flame of a faulty candle.

And we hurried down the wide stone stairs
with a clirr of spurr chains
on stone. And we thought
when the cocks crew
that the ghosts of a dead dawn
would rise and be off. But they stayed
under the window, crouched on the staircase,
the window now the colour of morning.

The colonel slept in the bed of Sully,
slept on: but we descended
and saw in a niche in the white wall
a Virgin and child, serene
who were stone: we saw sycamore:
three aged mages
scattering gifts of gold.
But when the wind blew, there were autumn odours
and the shadowed trees
had the dapplings of young fawns.

And each day one died or another
died: each week we sent out thousands
that returned by hundreds
wounded or gassed. And those that died
we buried close to the old wall
within a stone's throw of Perigord
under the tower of the troubadours.

And because we had courage;
because there was courage and youth
ready to be wasted; because we endured
and were prepared for all the endurance;
we thought something must come of it:
that the Virgin would raise her child and smile;
the trees gather up their gold and go;
that courage would avail something
and something we had never lost
be regained through wastage, by dying,
by burying the others under the English tower.

The colonel slept on in the bed of Sully
under the ravelling curtains: the leaves fell
and were blown away: the young men rotted
under the shadow of the tower
in a land of small clear silent streams
where the coming on of evening is
the letting down of blue and azure veils
over the clear and silent streams
delicately bordered by poplars."

General "Black Jack" Pershing.

IN THE TRENCHES

1

Not that we are weary,
Not that we fear,
Not that we are lonely
Though never alone—
Not these, not these destroy us;
But that each rush and crash
Of mortar and shell,
Each cruel bitter shriek of bullet
That tears the wind like a blade,
Each wound on the breast of earth,
Of Demeter, our Mother,
Wound us also,
Sever and rend the fine fabric
Of the wings of our frail souls,
Scatter into dust the bright wings
Of Psyche!

2

Impotent,
How impotent is all this clamour,
This destruction and contest . . .
Night after night comes the moon
Haughty and perfect;
Night after night the Pleiades sing
And Orion swings his belt across the sky.
Night after night the frost
Crumbles the hard earth.

Soon the spring will drop flowers
And patient creeping stalk and leaf
Along these barren lines
Where the huge rats scuttle
And the hawk shrieks to the carrion crow.

Richard Aldington

FIELD MANOEUVRES
Outpost Duty

The long autumn grass under my body
Soaks my clothes with its dew;
Where my knees press into the ground
I can feel the damp earth.

In my nostrils is the smell of the crushed grass,
Wet pine-cones and bark.

Through the great bronze pine trunks
Glitters a silver segment of road.
Interminable squadrons of silver and blue horses
Pace in long ranks the blank fields of heaven.

There is no sound;
The wind hisses gently through the pine needles;
The flutter of a finch's wings about my head
Is like distant thunder,
And the shrill cry of a mosquito
Sounds loud and close.

I am "to fire at the enemy column
After it has passed"—
But my obsolete rifle, loaded with "blank",
Lies untouched before me,
My spirit follows after the gliding clouds,
And my lips murmur of the mother of beauty
Standing breast-high, in golden broom
Among the blue pine-woods!

Richard Aldington

RESENTMENT

Why should you try to crush me?
Am I so Christ-like?

You beat against me,
Immense waves, filthy with refuse.
I am the last upright of a smashed breakwater
But you shall not crush me
Though you bury me in foaming slime
And hiss your hatred about me.

You break over me, cover me;
I shudder at the contact;
Yet I pierce through you
And stand up, torn, dripping, shaken,
But whole and fierce.

Richard Aldington

PREPARATIONS FOR VICTORY

My soul, dread not the pestilence that hags
The valley; flinch not you, my body young,
At these great shouting smokes and snarling jags
Of fiery iron; as yet may not be flung
The dice that claims you. Manly move among
These ruins, and what you must do, do well;
Look, here are gardens, there mossed boughs are hung
With apples whose bright cheeks none might excel,
And there's a house as yet unshattered by a shell.

"I'll do my best," the soul makes sad reply,
"And I will mark the yet unmurdered tree,
The tokens of dear homes that court the eye,
And yet I see them not as I would see.
Hovering between, a ghostly enemy.
Sickens the light, and poisoned, withered, wan,
The least defiled turns desperate to me."
The body, poor unpitied Caliban,
Parches and sweats and grunts to win the name of Man.

Days or eternities like swelling waves
Surge on, and still we drudge in this dark maze;
The bombs and coils and cans by strings of slaves
Are borne to serve the coming day of days;
Pale sleep in slimy cellars scarce allays
With its brief blank the burden. Look, we lose;
The sky is gone, the lightless, drenching haze
Of rainstorm chills the bone; earth, air are foes,
The black fiend leaps brick-red as life's last picture goes.

Edmund Blunden

Edmund Blunden.

GOUZEAUCOURT: THE DECEITFUL CALM

How unpurposed, how inconsequential
Seemed those southern lines when in the pallor
    Of the dying winter
    First we went there!

Grass thin-waving in the wind approached them,
Red roofs in the near view feigned survival,
    Lovely mockers, when we
    There took over.

There war's holiday seemed, nor though at known times
Gusts of flame and jingling steel descended
    On the bare tracks, would you
    Picture death there.

Snow or rime-frost made a solemn silence,
Bluish darkness wrapped in dangerous safety;
    Old hands thought of tidy
    Living-trenches!

There it was, my dear, that I departed,
Scarce a simpler traitor ever! There, too,
    Many of you soon paid for
    That false mildness.

Edmund Blunden

TWO VOICES

"There's something in the air," he said
    In the farm parlour cool and bare;
Plain words, which in his hearers bred
    A tumult, yet in silence there
All waited; wryly gay, he left the phrase,
Ordered the march, and bade us go our ways.

"We're going South, man"; as he spoke
    The howitzer with huge ping-bang
Racked the light hut; as thus he broke
    The death-news, bright the skylarks sang;
He took his riding-crop and humming went
Among the apple-trees all bloom and scent.

Now far withdraws the roaring night
    Which wrecked our flower after the first
Of those two voices; misty light
    Shrouds Thiepval Wood and all its worst;
But still "There's something in the air" I hear,
And still "We're going South, man," deadly near.

Edmund Blunden

TO E. T.: 1917

You sleep too well—too far away,
For sorrowing word to soothe or wound;
Your very quiet seems to say
How longed-for a peace you have found.

Else, had not death so lured you on,
You would have grieved—'twixt joy and fear—
To know how my small loving son
Had wept for you, my dear.

Walter de la Mare
(E.T.—Edward Thomas)

THE ZONNEBEKE ROAD

Morning, if this late withered light can claim
Some kindred with that merry flame
Which the young day was wont to fling through space!
Agony stares from each grey face.
And yet the day is come; stand down! stand down!
Your hands unclasp from rifles while you can;
The frost has pierced them to the bended bone?
Why, see old Stevens there, that iron man,
Melting the ice to shave his grotesque chin!
Go ask him, shall we win?
I never liked this bay, some foolish fear
Caught me the first time that I came in here;
That dugout fallen in awakes, perhaps,
Some formless haunting of some corpse's chaps.
True, and wherever we have held the line,
There were such corners, seeming-saturnine
For no good cause.
            Now where Haymarket starts,
That is no place for soldiers with weak hearts;
The minenwerfers have it to the inch.
Look, how the snow-dust whisks along the road
Piteous and silly; the stones themselves must flinch
In this east wind; the low sky like a load
Hangs over, a dead-weight. But what a pain
Must gnaw where its clay cheek
Crushes the shell-chopped trees that fang the plain—
The ice-bound throat gulps out a gargoyle shriek.
That wretched wire before the village line
Rattles like rusty brambles or dead bine,
And there the daylight oozes into dun;
Black pillars, those are trees where roadways run.
Even Ypres now would warm our souls; fond fool,
Our tour's but one night old, seven more to cool!
O screaming dumbness, O dull clashing death,
Shreds of dead grass and willows, homes and men,
Watch as you will, men clench their chattering teeth
And freeze you back with that one hope, disdain.

Edmund Blunde

THE POET AND WAR

I sang the songs of red ripped-up vengeance,
And I sang the stillness of the lake with wooded bays,
But none came to join me,
Steep, lonely
As the cicada singing,
I sang my song for myself.
My footsteps fade already, slackening
In the sand of travail.
With weariness my eyes drop from me,
I am weary of comfortless fords,
Of crossing waters, girls and streets.
In the abyss I do not remember
The shield and the spear.
Round me the whispering birches,
Round me the wind's shadow.
I fall asleep to the sound of the harp
Of other men
For whom it joyfully spills.
I do not stir,
For every thought and deed
Darkens the purity of the world.

Albert Ehrenstein
Trans. Christopher Middleton

Idyll in liberated France.

STRANGE HELLS

There are strange Hells within the minds War made
Not so often, not so humiliatingly afraid
As one would have expected—the racket and fear guns made.

One Hell the Gloucester soldiers they quite put out;
Their first bombardment, when in combined black shout
Of fury, guns aligned, they ducked low their heads
And sang with diaphragms fixed beyond all dreads,
That tin and stretched-wire tinkle, that blither of tune;
"Après la guerre fini" till Hell all had come down,
Twelve-inch, six-inch, and eighteen pounders hammering Hell's thunders.

Where are they now on State-doles, or showing shop patterns
Or walking town to town sore in borrowed tatterns
Or begged. Some civic routine one never learns.
The heart burns—but has to keep out of face how heart burns.

Ivor Gurney

THE SILENT ONE

Who died on the wires, and hung there, one of two—
Who for his hours of life had chattered through
Infinite lovely chatter of Bucks accent:
Yet faced unbroken wires; stepped over, and went
A noble fool, faithful to his stripes—and ended.
But I weak, hungry, and willing only for the chance
Of line—to fight in the line, lay down under unbroken
Wires, and saw the flashes and kept unshaken,
Till the politest voice—a finicking accent, said:
"Do you think you might crawl through, there: there's a hole"
Darkness, shot at: I smiled, as politely replied—
"I'm afraid not, Sir." There was no hole no way to be seen
Nothing but chance of death, after tearing of clothes
Kept flat, and watched the darkness, hearing bullets whizzing—
And thought of music—and swore deep heart's deep oaths
(Polite to God) and retreated and came on again,
Again retreated—and a second time faced the screen.

Ivor Gurney

BALLADE

Bodies of comrade soldiers gleaming white
    Within the mill-pool where you float and dive
And lounge around part-clothed or naked quite;
    Beautiful shining forms of men alive,
    O living lutes stringed with the senses five
For Love's sweet fingers; seeing Fate afar,
    My very soul with Death for you must strive;
Because of you I loathe the name of War.

But O you piteous corpses yellow-black,
    Rotting unburied in the sunbeam's light,
With teeth laid bare by yellow lips curled back
    Most hideously; whose tortured souls took flight
    Leaving your limbs, all mangled by the fight,
In attitudes of horror fouler far
    Than dreams which haunt a devil's brain at night;
Because of you I loathe the name of War.

Mothers and maids who loved you, and the wives
    Bereft of your sweet presences; yea, all
Who knew you beautiful, and those small lives
    Made of that knowledge; O, and you who call
    For life (but vainly now) from that dark hall
Where wait the Unborn, and the loves which are
    In future generations to befall;
Because of you I loathe the name of War.

L'ENVOI

Prince Jesu, hanging stark upon a tree
    Crucified as the malefactore are
That man and man henceforth should brothers be;
    Because of you I loathe the name of War.

F. W. Harvey

MESOPOTAMIA

They shall not return to us, the resolute, the young,
    The eager and whole-hearted whom we gave:
But the men who left them thriftily to die in their own dung,
    Shall they come with years and honour to the grave?

They shall not return to us, the strong men coldly slain
    In sight of help denied from day to day:
But the men who edged their agonies and chid them in their pain,
    Are they too strong and wise to put away?

Our dead shall not return to us while Day and Night divide—
    Never while the bars of sunset hold.
But the idle-minded overlings who quibbled while they died,
    Shall they thrust for high employments as of old?

Shall we only threaten and be angry for an hour?
    When the storm is ended shall we find
How softly but how swiftly they have sidled back to power
    By the favour and contrivance of their kind?

Even while they soothe us, while they promise large amends,
    Even while they make a show of fear,
Do they call upon their debtors, and take counsel with their friends,
    To confirm and re-establish each career?

Their lives cannot repay us—their death could not undo—
    The shame that they have laid upon our race.
But the slothfulness that wasted and the arrogance that slew,
    Shall we leave it unabated in its place?

Rudyard Kipling

PICNIC
July 1917

We lay and ate sweet hurt-berries
    In the bracken of Hurt Wood.
Like a quire of singers singing low
    The dark pines stood.

Behind us climbed the Surrey hills,
    Wild, wild in greenery;
At our feet the downs of Sussex broke
    To an unseen sea.

And life was bound in a still ring,
    Drowsy, and quiet, and sweet . . .
When heavily up the south-east wind
    The great guns beat.

We did not wince, we did not weep,
    We did not curse or pray;
We drowsily heard, and someone said,
    "They sound clear today".

We did not shake with pity and pain,
    Or sicken and blanch white.
We said, "If the wind's from over there
    There'll be rain tonight".

Once pity we knew, and rage we knew,
    And pain we knew, too well,
As we stared and peered dizzily
    Through the gates of hell.

But now hell's gates are an old tale;
    Remote the anguish seems;
The guns are muffled and far away,
    Dreams within dreams.

And far and far are Flanders mud,
    And the pain of Picardy;
And the blood that runs there runs beyond
    The wide waste sea.

We are shut about by guarding walls:
    (We have built them lest we run
Mad from dreaming of naked fear
    And of black things done).

We are ringed all round by guarding walls,
    So high, they shut the view.
Not all the guns that shatter the world
    Can quite break through.

Oh, guns of France, oh, guns of France,
    Be still, you crash in vain. . . .
Heavily up the south wind throb
    Dull dreams of pain, . . .

Be still, be still, south wind, lest your
    Blowing should bring the rain. . . .
We'll lie very quiet on Hurt Hill,
    And sleep once again.

Oh, we'll lie quite still, nor listen nor look,
    While the earth's bounds reel and shake,
Lest, battered too long, our walls and we
    Should break . . . should break. . . .

Rose Macaulay

DISABLED

He sat in a wheeled chair, waiting for dark,
And shivered in his ghastly suit of grey,
Legless, sewn short at elbow. Through the park
Voices of boys rang saddening like a hymn,
Voices of play and pleasure after day,
Till gathering sleep had mothered them from him.

About this time Town used to swing so gay
When glow-lamps budded in the light blue trees,
And girls glanced lovelier as the air grew dim,—
In the old times, before he threw away his knees.
Now he will never feel again how slim
Girls' waists are, or how warm their subtle hands.
All of them touch him like some queer disease.

There was an artist silly for his face,
For it was younger than his youth, last year.
Now, he is old; his back will never brace;
He's lost his colour very far from here,
Poured it down shell-holes till the veins ran dry,
And half his lifetime lapsed in the hot race
And leap of purple spurted from his thigh.

One time he liked a blood-smear down his leg,
After the matches, carried shoulder-high.
It was after football, when he'd drunk a peg,
He thought he'd better join.—He wonders why.
Someone had said he'd look a god in kilts,
That's why; and maybe, too, to please his Meg,
Aye, that was it, to please the giddy jilts
He asked to join. He didn't have to beg;
Smiling they wrote his lie: aged nineteen years.

Germans he scarcely thought of; all their guilt,
And Austria's, did not move him. And no fears
Of Fear came yet. He thought of jewelled hilts
For daggers in plaid socks; of smart salutes;
And care of arms; and leave; and pay arrears;
Esprit de corps; and hints for young recruits.
And soon, he was drafted out with drums and cheers.

Some cheered him home, but not as crowds cheer
    Goal.
Only a solemn man who brought him fruits
Thanked him; and then enquired about his soul.

Now, he will spend a few sick years in institutes,
And do what things the rules consider wise,
And take whatever pity they may dole.
Tonight he noticed how the women's eyes
Passed from him to the strong men that were whole.
How cold and late it is! Why don't they come
And put him into bed? Why don't they come?

Wilfred Owen

Right: *"Blinded for You!"*

EXPOSURE

Our brains ache, in the merciless iced east winds that knive us . . .
Wearied we keep awake because the night is silent . . .
Low, drooping flares confuse our memory of the salient, . . .
Worried by silence, sentries whisper, curious, nervous,
    But nothing happens.

Watching, we hear the mad gusts tugging on the wire,
Like twitching agonies of men among its brambles.
Northward, incessantly, the flickering gunnery rumbles,
Far off, like a dull rumour of some other war.
    What are we doing here?

The poignant misery of dawn begins to grow . . .
We only know war lasts, rain soaks, and clouds sag stormy.
Dawn massing in the east her melancholy army
Attacks once more in ranks on shivering ranks of gray,
    But nothing happens.

Sudden successive flights of bullets streak the silence.
Less deathly than the air that shudders black with snow
With sidelong flowing flakes that flock, pause, and renew
We watch them wandering up and down the wind's nonchalance,
    But nothing happens.

Pale flakes with fingering stealth come feeling for our faces
We cringe in holes, back on forgotten dreams, and stare, snow-dazed
Deep into grassier ditches. So we drowse, sun-dozed,
Littered with blossoms trickling where the blackbird fusses,
    —Is it that we are dying?

Slowly our ghosts drag home: glimpsing the sunk fires, glozed
With crusted dark-red jewels; crickets jingle there;
For hours the innocent mice rejoice: the house is theirs;
Shutters and doors, all closed: on us the doors are closed,—
    We turn back to our dying.

Since we believe not otherwise can kind fires burn;
Nor ever suns smile true on child, or field, or fruit.
For God's invincible spring our love is made afraid;
Therefore, not loath, we lie out here; therefore were born,
    For love of God seems dying.

To-night, this frost will fasten on this mud and us,
Shrivelling many hands, puckering foreheads crisp.
The burying-party, picks and shovels in shaking grasp,
Pause over half-known faces. All their eyes are ice,
    But nothing happens.

Wilfred Owen

"I am a soldier and unapt to weep
Or to exclaim on fortune's fickleness . . ."

*Thousands of men worked underground for two years to lay a million
pounds of high explosive for the greatest series of simultaneous
explosions in history at the Battle of Messines.*

SPRING OFFENSIVE

Halted against the shade of a last hill
They fed, and eased of pack-loads, were at ease;
And leaning on the nearest chest or knees
Carelessly slept.
                    But many there stood still
To face the stark blank sky beyond the ridge,
Knowing their feet had come to the end of the world.
Marvelling they stood, and watched the long grass swirled
By the May breeze, murmurous with wasp and midge;
And though the summer oozed into their veins
Like an injected drug for their bodies' pains,
Sharp on their souls hung the imminent ridge of grass,
Fearfully flashed the sky's mysterious glass.

Hour after hour they ponder the warm field
And the far valley behind where buttercups
Had blessed with gold their slow boots coming up;
When even the little brambles would not yield
But clutched and clung to them like sorrowing arms.
[All their strange day] they breathe like trees unstirred,

Till like a cold gust thrills the little word
At which each body and its soul begird
And tighten them for battle. No alarms
Of bugles, no high flags, no clamorous haste,—
Only a lift and flare of eyes that faced
The sun, like a friend with whom their love is done.
O larger shone that smile against the sun,—
Mightier than his whose bounty these have spurned.

So, soon they topped the hill, and raced together
Over an open stretch of herb and heather
Exposed. And instantly the whole sky burned
With fury against them; earth set sudden cups
In thousands for their blood; and the green slope
Chasmed and deepened sheer to infinite space.

Of them who running on that last high place
Breasted even the rapture of bullets, or went up
On the hot blast and fury of hell's upsurge,
Or plunged and fell away past this world's verge,
Some say God caught them even before they fell.

"Ils ne passeront pas."
Old soldiers never say die, they'll
simply block the way.

But what say such as from existence' brink
Ventured but drave too swift to sink,
The few who rushed in the body to enter hell,
And there out fiending all its fiends and flames
With superhuman inhumanities,
Long-famous glories, immemorial shames—
And crawling slowly back, have by degrees
Regained cool peaceful air in wonder—
Why speak not they of comrades that went under?

Wilfred Owen

THE DEAD-BEAT

He dropped,—more sullenly than wearily,
Lay stupid like a cod, heavy like meat,
And none of us could kick him to his feet;
—Just blinked at my revolver, blearily;
—Didn't appear to know a war was on,
Or see the blasted trench at which he stared.
"I'll do 'em in," he whined. "If this hand's spared,
I'll murder them, I will."

　　　A low voice said,
"It's Blighty, p'raps, he sees; his pluck's all gone,
Dreaming of all the valiant, that *aren't* dead:
Bold uncles, smiling ministerially;
Maybe his brave young wife, getting her fun
In some new home, improved materially.
It's not these stiffs have crazed him; nor the Hun."

We sent him down at last, out of the way.
Unwounded;—stout lad, too, before that strafe.
Malingering? Stretcher-bearers winked, "Not half!"

Next day I heard the Doc's well-whiskied laugh:
"That scum you sent last night soon died. Hooray!"

Wilfred Owen

THE HAPPY WARRIOR

His wild heart beats with painful sobs
his strain'd hands clench an ice-cold rifle
his aching jaws grip a hot parch'd tongue
his wide eyes search unconsciously.

He cannot shriek

Bloody saliva
dribbles down his shapeless jacket.

I saw him stab
and stab again
a well-killed Boche.

This is the happy warrior,
this is he . . .

Herbert Read

WINTER WARFARE

Colonel Cold strode up the Line
　　　(tabs of rime and spurs of ice);
stiffened all that met his glare:
　　　horses, men, and lice.

Visited a forward post,
　　　left them burning, ear to foot;
fingers stuck to biting steel,
　　　toes to frozen boot.

Stalked on into No Man's Land,
　　　turned the wire to fleecy wool,
iron stakes to sugar sticks
　　　snapping at a pull.

Those who watched with hoary eyes
　　　saw two figures gleaming there;
Hauptmann Kälte, Colonel Cold,
　　　gaunt in the grey air.

Stiffly, tinkling spurs they moved,
　　　glassy-eyed, with glinting heel
stabbing those who lingered there
　　　torn by screaming steel.

Edgell Rickword

Isaac Rosenberg.

"A WORM FED ON THE HEART OF CORINTH"

A worm fed on the heart of Corinth,
Babylon and Rome:
Not Paris raped tall Helen,
But this incestuous worm,
Who lured her vivid beauty
To his amorphous sleep.
England! famous as Helen
Is thy betrothal sung
To him the shadowless,
More amorous than Solomon.

Isaac Rosenberg

GIRL TO SOLDIER ON LEAVE

I love you—Titan lover,
My own storm-days' Titan.
Greater than the son of Zeus,
I know whom I would choose.

Titan—my splendid rebel—
The old Prometheus
Wanes like a ghost before your power—
His pangs were joys to yours.

Pallid days arid and wan
Tied your soul fast.
Babel-cities' smoky tops
Pressed upon your growth

Weary gyves. What were you
But a word in the brain's ways,
Or the sleep of Circe's swine?
One gyve holds you yet.

It held you hiddenly on the Somme
Tied from my heart at home.
O must it loosen now? I wish
You were bound with the old old gyves.

Love! you love me—your eyes
Have looked through death at mine.
You have tempted a grave too much.
I let you—I repine.

Isaac Rosenberg

RETURNING, WE HEAR THE LARKS

Sombre the night is.
And though we have our lives, we know
What sinister threat lurks there.

Dragging these anguished limbs, we only know
This poison-blasted track opens on our camp—
On a little safe sleep.

But hark! joy—joy—strange joy.
Lo! heights of night ringing with unseen larks.
Music showering on our upturned list'ning faces.

Death could drop from the dark
As easily as song—
But song only dropped,
Like a blind man's dreams on the sand
By dangerous tides,
Like a girl's dark hair for she dreams no ruin lies there,
Or her kisses where a serpent hides.

Isaac Rosenberg

"THEY"

The Bishop tells us: "When the boys come back
They will not be the same; for they'll have fought
In a just cause: they lead the last attack
On Anti-Christ; their comrades' blood has bought
New right to breed an honourable race.
They have challenged Death and dared him face to face."

"We're none of us the same!" the boys reply.
For George lost both his legs; and Bill's stone blind;
Poor Jim's shot through the lungs and like to die;
And Bert's gone syphilitic; you'll not find
A chap who's served that hasn't found *some* change."
And the Bishop said: "The ways of God are strange!"

Siegfried Sassoon

LAMENTATIONS

I found him in the guard-room at the Base.
From the blind darkness I had heard his crying
And blundered in. With puzzled, patient face
A sergeant watched him; it was no good trying
To stop it; for he howled and beat his chest.
And, all because his brother had gone west,
Raved at the bleeding war; his rampant grief
Moaned, shouted, sobbed, and choked, while he was kneeling
Half-naked on the floor. In my belief
Such men have lost all patriotic feeling.

Siegfried Sassoon

A WORKING PARTY

Three hours ago he blundered up the trench,
Sliding and poising, groping with his boots;
Sometimes he tripped and lurched against the walls
With hands that pawed the sodden bags of chalk.
He couldn't see the man who walked in front;
Only he heard the drum and rattle of feet
Stepping along barred trench boards, often splashing
Wretchedly where the sludge was ankle-deep.

Voices would grunt "Keep to your right—make way!"
When squeezing past some men from the front-line:
White faces peered, puffing a point of red;
Candles and braziers glinted through the chinks
And curtain-flaps of dug-outs; then the gloom
Swallowed his sense of sight; he stooped and swore
Because a sagging wire had caught his neck.

A flare went up; the shining whiteness spread
And flickered upward, showing nimble rats
And mounds of glimmering sand-bags, bleached with rain;
Then the slow silver moment died in dark.
The wind came posting by with chilly gusts
And buffeting at corners, piping thin.
And dreary through the crannies; rifle-shots
Would split and crack and sing along the night,
And shells came calmly through the drizzling air
To burst with hollow bang below the hill.
Three hours ago he stumbled up the trench;
Now he will never walk that road again:
He must be carried back, a jolting lump
Beyond all need of tenderness and care.

Monster of the cathedral:
the German Crown Prince.

THE GENERAL

"Good-morning; good-morning!" the General said
When we met him last week on our way to the Line.
Now the soldiers he smiled at are most of 'em dead,
And we're cursing his staff for incompetent swine.
"He's a cheery old card," grunted Harry to Jack
As they slogged up to Arras with rifle and pack.

But he did for them both by his plan of attack.

Siegfried Sassoon

He was a young man with a meagre wife
And two small children in a Midland town;
He showed their photographs to all his mates,
And they considered him a decent chap
Who did his work and hadn't much to say,
And always laughed at other people's jokes
Because he hadn't any of his own.

That night when he was busy at his job
Of piling bags along the parapet,
He thought how slow time went, stamping his feet
And blowing on his fingers, pinched with cold.
He thought of getting back by half-past twelve,
And tot of rum to send him warm to sleep
In draughty dug-out frowsty with the fumes
Of coke, and full of snoring weary men.

He pushed another bag along the top,
Craning his body outward; then a flare
Gave one white glimpse of No Man's Land and wire;
And as he dropped his head the instant split
His startled life with lead, and all went out.

Siegfried Sassoon

SONG-BOOKS OF THE WAR

In fifty years, when peace outshines
Remembrance of the battle lines,
Adventurous lads will sigh and cast
Proud looks upon the plundered past.
On summer morn or winter's night
Their hearts will kindle for the fight,

Reading a snatch of soldier-song,
Savage and jaunty, fierce and strong;
And through the angry marching rhymes
Of blind regret and haggard mirth,
They'll envy us the dazzling times
When sacrifice absolved our earth.

Some ancient man with silver locks
Will lift his weary face to say:
"War was a fiend who stopped our clocks
Although we met him grim and gay."
And then he'll speak of Haig's last drive,
Marvelling that any came alive
Out of the shambles that men built
And smashed, to cleanse the world of guilt.
But the boys, with grim and sidelong glance,
Will think, "Poor grandad's day is done,"
And dream of lads who fought in France
And lived in time to share the fun.

Siegfried Sassoon

*The bare essentials of a
soldier's kitbag.*

REPRESSION OF WAR EXPERIENCE

Now light the candles; one; two; there's a moth;
What silly beggars they are to blunder in
And scorch their wings with glory, liquid flame—
No, no, not that,—it's bad to think of war
When thoughts you've gagged all day come back to scare you;
And it's been proved that soldiers don't go mad
Unless they lose control of ugly thoughts
That drive them out to jabber among the trees.

Now light your pipe; look, what a steady hand.
Draw a deep breath; stop thinking; count fifteen,
And you're as right as rain. . .
                      Why won't it rain? . . .
I wish there'd be a thunder-storm to-night,
With bucketsful of water to sluice the dark
And make the roses hang their dripping heads.
Books; what a jolly company they are,
Standing so quiet and patient on their shelves,
Dressed in dim brown, and black, and white, and green;
And every kind of colour. Which will you read?
Come on; O *do* read something; they're so wise.
I tell you all the wisdom of the world
Is waiting for you on those shelves; and yet
You sit and gnaw your nails, and let your pipe out,
And listen to the silence: on the ceiling
There's one big, dizzy moth that bumps and flutters;
And in the breathless air outside the house
The garden waits for something that delays.
There must be crowds of ghosts among the trees,—
Not people killed in battle,—they're in France,—
But horrible shapes in shrouds—old men who died
Slow, natural deaths,—old men with ugly souls,
Who wore their bodies out with nasty sins.
You're quiet and peaceful, summering safe at home;
You'd never think there was a bloody war on! . . .
O yes, you would . . . why, you can hear the guns.
Hark! Thud, thud, thud,—quite soft . . . they never cease—
Those whispering guns—O Christ, I want to go out
And screech at them to stop—I'm going crazy;
I'm going stark, staring mad because of the guns.

Siegfried Sassoon

Tommies round a lamp in a dug-out.

THE REAR-GUARD

(Hindenburg Line, April, 1917)

Groping along the tunnel, step by step,
He winked his prying torch with patching glare
From side to side, and sniffed the unwholesome air.

Tins, boxes, bottles, shapes too vague to know,
A mirror smashed, the mattress from a bed;
And he, exploring fifty feet below
The rosy gloom of battle overhead.

Tripping, he grabbed the wall; saw some one lie
Humped at his feet, half-hidden by a rug,
And stooped to give the sleeper's arm a tug.
"I'm looking for headquarters." No reply.
"God blast your neck!" (For days he'd had no sleep,)
"Get up and guide me through this stinking place."
Savage, he kicked a soft, unanswering heap,
And flashed his beam across the livid face
Terribly glaring up, whose eyes yet wore
Agony dying hard ten days before;
And fists of fingers clutched a blackening wound.

Alone he staggered on until he found
Dawn's ghost that filtered down a shafted stair
To the dazed, muttering creatures underground
Who hear the boom of shells in muffled sound.
At last, with sweat of horror in his hair,
He climbed through darkness to the twilight air,
Unloading hell behind him step by step.

Siegfried Sassoon

DREAMERS

Soldiers are citizens of death's gray land,
Drawing no dividend from time's to-morrows.
In the great hour of destiny they stand,
　Each with his feuds and jealousies and sorrows.
Soldiers are sworn to action; they must win
　Some flaming fatal climax with their lives.
Soldiers are dreamers; when the guns begin
　They think of firelit homes, clean beds, and wives.

I see them in foul dug-outs, gnawed by rats,
　And in the ruined trenches, lashed with rain,
Dreaming of things they did with balls and bats,
　And mocked by hopeless longing to regain
Bank-holidays, and picture shows, and spats,
　And going to the office in the train.

Siegfried Sassoon

1918

"What we demand in this war . . . is nothing peculiar to ourselves. It is that the world be made fit and safe to live in . . . All the peoples of the world are in effect partners in this interest."

Woodrow Wilson, at a session of the Congress, 8th January 1918

"There was no cheering or excitement amongst the men. They seemed too tired, and no one seemed able to realize that it was all over."

Diary entry for 11th November 1918, Brigadier George Elkington

From the Central Powers' point of view, in August 1914 success in the Great War could be achieved by dealing with the French before the Russians had a chance to mobilize. In this they failed. At the beginning of 1918, with the Russians out of the war, victory could be achieved only by utilizing the temporary superiority in numbers they enjoyed as a result of the Russian collapse and decisively defeating the British and French armies on the Western Front before the U.S. troops could arrive in strength. A major offensive by the Germans was therefore widely discussed as a more than likely possibility during the opening weeks of 1918; among the Allied troops it had been a topic of conversation and jokes since Christmas:

> *"We have it on the best authority that William Hohenzollern has a little boat ready, with steam up, to cut it to Sweden . . . Up to now the luck has generally been with the Huns, but it looks as if it were going to leave them in the New Year . . . We've heard so many tales from Hunland about what he's going to do to us now that he's fixed Russia, that it makes us think that he's trying to forget what we are going to do to him. It is still our firm opinion that any Hun could be bought for a tin of bully and a slice of bread. Anyway, we feel inclined to get mixed up with the prophets Elijah, John the Baptist and Horatio Bottomley, and prophesy the general bust up of the Hun at no very remote date. Say, September next."*

> *(The Wipers Times, 22nd January 1918)*

The new year opened with the Allies very much on the defensive. Their offensives in 1917 had achieved little real advance, and they suffered from a serious lack of unity among the commanders. It would still be months before U.S. military strength could be exerted effectively on the Western Front, meanwhile German U-boats threatened the supply lines across the Atlantic.

U.S. strength, however, was building up: the army now totalled four million men, with 200,000 officers. General John Joseph ("Black Jack") Pershing commanded the U.S. Expeditionary Force, and his policy was to keep it out of battle until assembled in sufficient numbers to intervene decisively. Training concentrated on expert marksmanship, and instilling into the men the spirit of the offensive—moving film was extensively used in their training programme.

The strength of the Central Powers was at a low ebb; the British blockade was taking its toll, Austria was nearly exhausted, Turkey and Bulgaria were nearing collapse. Yet despite this, in the spring of 1918 the Germans were willing and able to take the offensive. Ludendorff's plans to win a decisive victory in the west were to be achieved by driving a wedge between the British and the French. He recognized that they had

"The sensations of going over the top are about as exhilarating
as those dreams of falling over a precipice . . ."
Following page:
"I'm back again from hell
With loathsome thoughts to sell;
Secrets of death to tell;
And horrors from the abyss . . ."

"How impotent is all this clamour,
This destruction and contest . . ."

"And the singers are the chaps
Who are going to die perhaps.
O sing, marching men,
Till the valleys ring again . . ."

The British magazine Punch's *message for the New Year was
not couched in a spirit of premature jubilation, but appealed
to all at home for fortitude and endurance.*

different priorities: for the British, their lines of communication to the
Channel ports; for the French, the safety of Paris.

THE KAISER'S OFFENSIVE

The first German attack came at the end of March with five hours of
shelling on the Front from the Oise to the Scarpe. Then the massed
German divisions advanced, the attack helped by thick, white fog which

handicapped the defending infantry. Gough's outnumbered Fifth Army gave up ground, but elsewhere German gains were limited and, with the struggle to keep the troops supplied when travelling over an area that had been so devastated, the momentum of advance was lost. The Allies were helped by eight U.S. divisions which Pershing had supplied to aid the emergency, and this stage of the German offensive came to an end by 5th April. After this engagement, in which it had been clear that Pétain's main concern was for protecting Paris, the British appealed for a commander who would fight with them, and in response Foch was made Generalissimo supreme commander of Allied Forces in France.

The second German offensive of the year—the Lys offensive—was launched against the British along a narrow front in Flanders. This was a serious threat to the Channel ports in which the Germans made good headway, advancing more than halfway to Hazebrouk, held only by fierce opposition at the forest of Nieppe. This was the context for Haig's famous Order of the Day to the British Expeditionary Force on 12th April:

*German reservists sent to the Front – Ludendorff
could not compete with the numbers of U.S. troops
flooding into Europe during 1918.*

Colonel-General Paul von Hindenburg.

"Many of us are now tired. To those I would say that victory will belong to the side which holds out the longest . . . There is no other course open to us but to fight it out! Every position must be held to the last man: there must be no retirement. With our backs to the wall and believing in the justice of our cause, each one of us must fight on to the end. The safety of our Homes and the Freedom of mankind alike depend upon the conduct of each one of us at this critical moment."

Luckily for the British the Germans failed to press home their advantage. Discipline in the German armies had relaxed, and pillaging (especially at Merville) slowed down their advance; secondly, the troops were discouraged by rumours of French reinforcements. Although (much to Haig's annoyance) these never materialized, the British were reinforced by vigorous divisions from Italy and Palestine which contrasted favourably to the dispirited troops from the Eastern Front that were joining the Germans. Another factor at this time, helping the scales of the conflict to tip in the Allies' favour, was the arrival of U.S. troops that now flooded in at the rate of 250,000 a month.

Firing a heavy howitzer in France.

The Germans' third attack of 1918 came on the Aisne, in May. Taking the French by surprise, they crossed the river and within a few days had reached the Marne—the closest they had got to Paris since the heady days of their initial advance in 1914. This success was followed, however, by the first major U.S. engagement of the war at Cantigny, at which the Germans were dealt a resounding blow. The Germans had reached Château-Thierry, 40 miles from the French capital, when their advance was halted and the 2nd and 3rd U.S. divisions drove them back. In the U.S. counterattack the Germans were then forced from their positions at Vaux, Bouresches and Belleau Wood. Casualties on both sides were high.

A pattern was beginning to be established: German attack, initial success and advance, but then Allied defences halting and repelling the offensive. In July, French, Italian and U.S. troops successfully frustrated the German attempts to move towards Reims and Compiègne, and at the Second Battle of the Marne which followed, the German advance was brought to a halt after German bridges and supply lines had been wrecked by attacks from aircraft and artillery. The Germans prepared to withdraw from the salient.

TURNING OF THE TIDE

Between 18th July and 5th August came the Aisne-Marne offensive which marked the turning point of the tide of the war. The threat to Paris was removed, and the Marne Salient no longer existed. In recognition of Foch's successful co-ordination of Allied plans Clemenceau promoted him to Marshal of France, but the major reason for the changes in fortune was the advent of 300,000 high quality U.S. troops per month. Ludendorff could not compete with this; he had lost half a million troops in five months fighting.

On 8th August the Amiens offensive was launched, and the steady Allied advance began. By the end of August, the Germans had retired to the Hindenburg Line. They had lost 100,000 men during the Amiens offensive, including 30,000 prisoners. Ludendorff described 8th August as a "black day for the German Army". "The war must be ended", he declared.

The Allies continued to advance and take prisoners throughout September and at the beginning of October German resistance began to crack. The German Chancellor, Prince Max von Baden, sent a message to President Wilson indicating Germany's wish for an armistice, but, after some discussions, Wilson's reply was that the Allies would not negotiate with the Kaiser's military dictatorship. Continued acts of cruelty, pillage and destruction committed by German soldiers during the retreat across France handicapped the peace negotiations, and Wilson's final reply to the Chancellor on 14th October was that no armistice could be considered while Germans committed "illegal and inhuman practices . . . acts of inhumanity, spoliation and desolation", which the Allies justly regarded "with horror and with burning hearts".

Some of the 30,000 Germans captured at Amiens – a great British victory, but a "black day for the German Army".

CEASE FIRE

In the meantime the Allies continued to advance, signing an armistice with Austria-Hungary on 3rd November. In Germany, the war effort had clearly collapsed. The High Seas Fleet mutinied at Kiel, a republic was proclaimed in Bavaria, and, in the face of revolution in Berlin, Kaiser Wilhelm II abdicated and fled to Holland. After this, Ludendorff resigned to enable an armistice to be negotiated, and in due course a delegation was conveyed to Marshal Foch's railway carriage head-quarters at Rethondes. The only option the Germans were given for obtaining an armistice was to accept Wilson's Fourteen Points and, eventually, they had to agree. At 11 a.m. on 11th November the "cease fire" sounded over the entire Front. Artillery went on firing right up to 10.59 a.m. but then it stopped abruptly. The Great War was at an end.

Germans threw their helmets and rifles in the air and came over to shake hands, but for some the end was sudden and unexpected and they found it hard to believe. Further back from the front lines there was great willingness to demonstrate joy and to celebrate, but closer to the Front the news was received with stupefaction or indifference, many of the rank and file simply could not imagine life without the war. Neverthe-less, the vast relief which was felt by most was expressed in the

*Artist's impression of General Foch at
Cassel, 1915. In 1918 Foch became overall commander
of the Allied armies on the Western Front.*

*France's demands for vengeance against Germany dominated
the preparations for the Versailles Conference.*

extraordinary nature of the welcome given to President Wilson when he
came to help make the peace. To the huge crowds that turned out to see
him as he arrived in Paris on 14th December, he seemed "the Saviour
from the New World". Herbert Hoover recorded:

> *"To them no such man of moral or political power and no such evangel of
> peace had appeared since Christ preached the Sermon on the Mount.
> Everywhere men believed that a new era had come to all mankind."*

A POET SET FREE BY DEATH

In December 1918 Isaac Rosenberg had again been declared fit for active
service by the army physicians. Once discharged from hospital, he
returned to the trenches on the Western Front and in March was placed
in the reserve brigade. He knew that the stress of the Front was bringing
him near to breaking point. Two poems he wrote at this stage—*The
Destruction of Jerusalem by the Babylonian Hordes*, and *The Burning of the
Temple*—although based on biblical subjects, reflect the strains of the
Great War. He hoped that he might obtain a transfer to the Near East,

serving in the Jewish Battalion. Most of his colleagues whom he remembered from earlier days in the 11th King's Own Lancasters had been killed, Rosenberg and the few others who remained were detailed to the 1st King's Own Lancasters. On 1st April, while on night patrol, he was shot and killed; he was aged 27.

Before F.R. Leavis, Rosenberg's qualities had not really been recognized by the literary establishment. Leavis was full of admiration:

> *"genius is the word for Rosenberg . . . the total effect (of reading his poetry) should be not only the recognised enrichment of the English language by a dozen pages of great poetry, but also the enrichment of tradition by a new legend."*

As Joseph Cohen wrote in his moving biography of Rosenberg, *Journey to the Trenches*, if Brooke's death in 1915 became the symbol of the "brave sacrifices of the young, then Rosenberg's death on All Fool's Day in 1918 became the symbol of the futility of such sacrifices".

SASSOON IN EGYPT

In January, Siegfried Sassoon was sent to Limerick before embarking for Egypt. He enjoyed the rest cure in Ireland, hunting, socializing and reading, but he knew that this "peace of mind; freedom from all care; the jollity of health and good companions" was a "drugged peace", an evasion of reality. From the same period dates the poem *Journey's End*.

> "Saved by unnumbered miracles of chance,
> You'll stand, with war's unholiness behind,
> Its years, like gutted villages in France,
> Done with; its shell-bursts drifting out of mind.
> Then will you look upon your time to be,
> Like a man staring over a foreign town,
> Who hears strange bells, and knows himself set free;
> And quietly to the twinkling lights goes gladly down,
> To find new faces in the streets, and win
> Companionship from life's warm firelit inn."

This was probably addressed to Lieutenant W.M. Morgan, one of the poet's regimental companions, it shows an ability not only to dwell on the past, but to think to a future which is better than the present.

When Sassoon learned that he was being sent to Egypt, he weighed up the position. In favour of going he found it was a new country, where the conditions were not so trying, and there was less chance of being killed than in France. Among the books he took with him to Egypt were *War and Peace*, *The Woodlanders*, and Henri Barbusse's *Le Feu*. He resolved to give up the idea of writing "picturesque" poems about his experiences:

*"Then jabbering echoes stampede in the slatting wood,
Ember-black the gibbet trees like bones or thorns protrude
From the poisonous smoke . . ."*

"Must concentrate on the tragic, emotional, human episodes in the drama. Shall I find them out here? Little Welsh officers in a warm-climate side-show. An urbane existence. Like this dock, with its glassy dark water, and warm night—stars, and gold moon, and the dark ships . . . safe in port once more. No tragedy. Nothing heroic. I must have the heroic. So good-bye to amiable efforts at nature-poems. If I write I'll write tense and bitter and proud and pitiful."

Tolstoy's battle pictures, he notes in his diary, helped him remember his own experiences, probably the same was true of *Le Feu*. Reading *The Woodlanders*, he wrote, was "Like going into a cool parlour . . . after the heat and sweat of marching".

In April, the Egyptian base camp was visited by Lena Ashwell's Concert Party, and the poem that this inspired Sassoon to write was published in the *New Statesman* on 17th August:

"They are gathering round . . .
Out of the twilight; over the grey-blue sand,
Shoals of low-jargoning men drift inward to the sound,—
The jangle and throb of a piano . . . tum-ti-tum. . . .
Drawn by a lamp, they come
Out of the glimmering lines of their tents, over the shuffling sand.

O sing us the songs, the songs of our own land,
You warbling ladies in white.
Dimness conceals the hunger in our faces,
This wall of faces risen out of the night,
These eyes that keep their memories of the places
So long beyond their sight.

Jaded and gay, the ladies sing; and the chap in brown
Tilts his grey hat; jaunty and lean and pale,
He rattles the keys . . . some actor-bloke from town . . .
'God send you home'; and then 'A long, long trail';
'I hear you calling me'; and 'Dixieland' . . .
Sing slowly . . . now the chorus . . . one by one.
We hear them, drink them; till the concert's done.
Silent, I watch the shadowy mass of soldiers stand.
Silent, they drift away, over the glimmering sand."

*"But why don't the bastards come –
Bearers! – stret-cher bear-errs! . . ."*

Sassoon, as Rosenberg had been, was still under considerable stress, this much he admitted in his diary in April:

> "if I am killed this year, I shall be free. Selfishness longs for escape, and dreads the burden that is so infinitely harder to carry than three years, two years, one year ago. The simplicity that I see in some of the men is the one candle in my darkness. The one flower in all this arid sunshine. Half-baked aspirations and reasonings are no good. I will not go mad."

Early in May he sailed on the S.S. *Malwa*, with over 3,000 other troops, for the Western Front. When he returned to France he felt like a ghost, coming back to the familiar country. The war was 40 miles away and he could not think it would end that year.

A LUCKY ESCAPE

On 13th July, Sassoon was just returning from a patrol in No Man's Land when he was shot in the head by one of his own sergeants, who mistook him for an advancing German. The incident is recounted in *Sherston's Progress*:

> "With my tin hat in my hand I stood up and turned for a moment to look back at the German line. A second later I was down again, half stunned by a terrific blow on the head. It seemed to me that there was a very large hole in the right side of my skull. I felt, and believed, that I was as good as dead . . . While the blood poured from my head, I was intensely aware of everything around me—the clear sky and the ripening corn . . . I saw it all as though for the last time."

He was hospitalized at the base and then sent back to England, to the Red Cross Hospital at Lancaster Gate in London. His volume of poetry, *Counter Attack*, was published in July while he was recovering, and was well received by the press. During his convalescence he enjoyed socializing with leading members of the literary and artistic circles— Edward Marsh, "Robbie" Ross, Maurice Baring, Clive Bell, Ottoline Morrell, Arnold Bennett, Maynard Keynes, Desmond MacCarthy, T.E. Lawrence and the Sitwells. He went to Max Gate, Thomas Hardy's house at Dorchester, and found England's greatest living novelist and poet shy, but hospitable, and the better he got to know him the more "lovable" he became. While Sassoon was in hospital, he had a visit from Wilfred Owen. It was the last time they were to meet.

THE "INSENSIBILITY" OF WAR

On 23rd January, Owen had been among the guests at Robert Graves' wedding at St. James's, Piccadilly. He bought Graves a present of 11

Apostle Spoons. The 12th, he joked, had been court-martialled for cowardice and was awaiting execution. In March, Owen was transferred to the Northern Command Depot at Ripon, and there he wrote *The Send Off*, a fine example of the quintessential Owen—a deceptively gentle surface quality which thinly masks the harsh realities he has observed. It is a superb answer to "Smilin' Through", "There's a Long Long Trail", and other such sentimental lyrics. He turns back on his readers their own pastoral-nostalgia to grim effect:

"Down the close darkening lanes they sang their way
To the siding-shed,
And lined the train with faces grimly gay.

Their breasts were stuck all white with wreath and spray
As men's are, dead.

Dull porters watched them, and a casual tramp
Stood staring hard,
Sorry to miss them from the upland camp.

Then, unmoved, signals nodded, and a lamp
Winked to the guard.

So secretly, like wrongs hushed-up, they went.
They were not ours:
We never heard to which front these were sent;

Nor there if they yet mock what women meant
Who gave them flowers.

Shall they return to beating of great bells
In wild train-loads?
A few, a few, too few for drums and yells,

May creep back, silent, to village wells,
Up half-known roads."

Through "Robbie" Ross, Wilfred Owen was introduced to Osbert Sitwell, who left a fine portrait of him in *Noble Essences*. Sitwell recorded that Owen was sturdy and of medium height, wearing his uniform. His face was broad and unusual in the width of the eyes and forehead. He seemed young for his age and was rather shy:

"He had the eager, supple good manners of the sensitive, and was eager and receptive, quick to see a point and smile. His voice . . . A soft modulation, even-toned, but with a warmth in it . . . a well proportioned voice that signified a sense of justice and compassion."

The contact with Sitwell was to have important consequences for Owen's reputation as a poet. At this time he was busy working up the final version of the poem we now know as *Mental Cases*.

"Who are these? Why sit they here in twilight?
Wherefore rock they, purgatorial shadows,
Drooping tongues from jaws that slob their relish,
Baring teeth that leer like skulls' teeth wicked?
Stroke on stroke of pain,—but what slow panic,
Gouged these chasms round their fretted sockets?
Ever from their hair and through their hands' palms
Misery swelters. Surely we have perished
Sleeping, and walk hell; but who these hellish?

—These are men whose minds the Dead have ravished.
Memory fingers in their hair of murders,
Multitudinous murders they once witnessed.
Wading sloughs of flesh these helpless wander,
Treading blood from lungs that had loved laughter.
Always they must see these things and hear them,
Batter of guns and shatter of flying muscles,
Carnage incomparable, and human squander
Rucked too thick for these men's extrication.

Therefore still their eyeballs shrink tormented
Back into their brains, because on their sense
Sunlight seems a blood-smear; night comes blood-black;
Dawn breaks open like a wound that bleeds afresh.
—Thus their heads wear this hilarious, hideous,
Awful falseness of set-smiling corpses.
—Thus their hands are plucking at each other;
Picking at the rope-knouts of their scourging,
Snatching after us who smote them, brother,
Pawing us who dealt them war and madness."

Charles Kenneth Scott-Moncrieff, a captain in the King's Own Scottish Borderers, who had been invalided home and had been posted to a staff job, met Owen, and showed the poem, then called *The Deranged*, to the Sitwells. They asked to see more of his work to consider it for inclusion in Edith Sitwell's annual Modernist anthology, *Wheels*. The edition of *Wheels* published in 1918 contained no poems by Owen, but the 1919 volume was dedicated posthumously to him. It included some of his finest work, thus introducing him to the discerning readership of new poetry.

In June, Owen began preparing a selection of his work for publication which he entitled *Disabled and Other Poems*. For this he drafted a Preface that has since become world famous.

"This book is not about heroes. English poetry is not yet fit to speak of them.

Nor is it about deeds, or lands, nor anything about glory, honour, might, majesty, dominion, or power, except War.

Above all I am not concerned with Poetry.

My subject is War, and the pity of War.

The Poetry is in the pity.

Yet these elegies are to this generation in no sense consolatory. They may be to the next. All a poet can do today is warn. That is why the true Poets must be truthful.

(If I thought the letter of this book would last, I might have used proper names; but if the spirit of it survives—survives Prussia—my ambition and those names will have achieved fresher fields than Flanders. . . .)"

INTO BATTLE ONCE MORE

At the end of August 1918, Owen was passed fit for active service overseas. He went to say goodbye to Siegfried Sassoon, who was still in hospital, then, on the way back to the Front, he wrote to him:

"I've been incoherent ever since I tried to say goodbye on the steps of Lancaster Gate. But everything is clear now; and I'm in hasty retreat towards the Front. Battle is easier here; and therefore you will stay and endure old men and women to the End, and wage the bitterer war and more hopeless."

On 31st August 1918, Owen reported to base camp, Etaples, and from there went to the reception depot at Amiens to await the arrival of the 2nd Manchester Regiment. During these few days, as U.S. troops launched their offensive at St. Mihiel and the Allied breakthrough in Bulgaria began, he wrote *Smile, Smile, Smile* (the ironic title borrowed from one of the most popular "jollying-along" songs of the Western Front).

Between 29th September and 3rd October Owen took part in the assault on the Beaurevoir-Fonsomme line with the 96th Brigade and the 5th Australian Division which was part of the Allies' advance. For his bravery here he was awarded the Military Cross:

"For conspicuous gallantry and devotion to duty in the attack on the Fonsomme Line on 1st and 2nd October 1918. On the Company Commander becoming a casualty, he assumed command and showed fine leadership and resisted heavy counterattack. He personally manipulated a captured enemy machine gun in an isolated position and inflicted considerable losses on the enemy. Throughout he behaved most gallantly."

"THE PITY OF WAR"

By the end of October it was clear to Owen that the German forces were collapsing. He was in action at the line for the last time on 29th October, at St. Souplet. In the last days of the month the battalion took over the line west of the Oise-Sambre Canal, close to Ors. An attack was planned to take place at dawn on 4th November. There was heavy rain during the night followed by mist. Against a hail of German machine gun fire that inflicted terrible casualties, the British troops effected the crossing of the canal. Wilfred Owen was walking among his men, congratulating them and encouraging them, when he was hit and killed. It was a terrible irony that his family received the telegram bearing the news of his death at the same time as the bells were ringing to welcome the news of the Armistice on 11th November.

Supporting troops, silhouetted against
a sombre sky, going up after a battle to
relieve the men in the front line.

The sands run out.

No scholar has more warmly brought Owen's life and work to public recognition, or summarized Owen's qualities better than Jon Stallworthy, who wrote in *Wilfred Owen: A Biography*:

"It is now possible to see that his gifts were not only gifts of genius, but other gifts that only the gods bestow. He came to the war with his imagination in large measure conditioned and prepared to receive and record the experiences of the trenches . . . He wrote more eloquently than other poets of the tragedy of boys killed in battle, because he felt that tragedy more acutely, and his later elegies spring from his earlier preoccupations as flowers from their stem."

"ALL QUIET ON THE WESTERN FRONT"

News of the end of the war was greeted with mixed feelings. Robert Graves, posted to a camp in Wales, recorded in *Goodbye to All That* that the news came at the same time that he heard of Wilfred Owen's death:

"Armistice-night hysteria did not touch our camp much, though some of the Canadians stationed there went down to Rhyl to celebrate in true overseas style. The news sent me out walking alone along the dyke above the marshes of Rhuddlan (an ancient battlefield, the Flodden of Wales) cursing and sobbing and thinking of the dead."

Siegfried Sassoon recorded this entry in his diary for 11th November 1918:

"I was walking in the water meadows by the river below Cuddesdon this morning—a quiet grey day. A jolly peal of bells was ringing from the village church, and the villagers were hanging little flags out of the windows of their thatched houses. The war is ended. It is impossible to realize. Oxford had much flag-waving also, and signs of demonstration.

I got to London about 6.30 and found masses of people in streets and congested tubes, all waving flags and making fools of themselves—an outburst of mob patriotism. It was a wretched wet night, and very mild. It is a loathsome ending to the loathsome tragedy of the last four years."

THE LAMENT OF THE DEMOBILISED

"Four years," some say consolingly. "Oh well,
What's that? You're young. And then it must have been
A very fine experience for you!"
And they forget
How others stayed behind and just got on—
Got on the better since we were away.
And we came home and found
They had achieved, and men revered their names,
But never mentioned ours;
And no one talked heroics now, and we
Must just go back and start again once more.
"You threw four years into the melting-pot—
Did you indeed!" these others cry. "Oh well,
The more fool you!"
And we're beginning to agree with them.

Vera Brittain

TO MY BROTHER
(In Memory of July 1st, 1916)

Your battle-wounds are scars upon my heart,
Received when in that grand and tragic "show"
      You played your part
      Two years ago,

And silver in the summer morning sun
I see the symbol of your courage glow—
      That Cross you won
      Two years ago.

Though now again you watch the shrapnel fly,
And hear the guns that daily louder grow,
      As in July
      Two years ago,

May you endure to lead the Last Advance,
And with your men pursue the flying foe,
      As once in France
      Two years ago.

Vera Brittain

Walter de la Mare.

HAPPY ENGLAND

Now each man's mind all Europe is:
      Boding and fear in dread array
Daze every heart: O grave and wise,
      Abide in hope the judgment day.

This war of millions in arms
      In myriad replica we wage;
Unmoved, then, Soul, by earth's alarms
      The dangers of the dark engage.

Remember happy England: keep
      For her bright cause thy latest breath;
Her peace that long hath lulled to sleep,
      May now exact the sleep of death.

Her woods and wilds, her loveliness,
      With harvest now are richly at rest;
Safe in her isled securities,
      Thy children's heaven is her breast.

O what a deep contented night
      The sun from out her Eastern seas
Would bring the dust which in her sight
      Had given its all for these!

Walter de la Mare

A SHORT POEM FOR ARMISTICE DAY

Gather or take fierce degree
trim the lamp set out for sea
here we are at the workmen's entrance
clock in and shed your eminence.

Notwithstanding, work it diverse ways
work it diverse days, multiplying four digestions
here we make artificial flowers
of paper tin and metal thread.

One eye one leg one arm one lung
a syncopated sick heart-beat
the record is not nearly worn
that weaves a background to our work.

I have no power therefore have patience
These flowers have no sweet scent
no lustre in the petal no increase
from fertilising flies and bees.

No seed they have no seed
their tendrils are of wire and grip
the buttonhole the lip
and never fade

And will not fade though life
and lustre go in genuine flowers
and men like flowers are cut
and wither on a stem

And will not fade a year or more
I stuck one in a candlestick
and there it clings about the socket
I have no power therefore have patience.

Herbert Read

GALA
To André Rouveyre

Skyrocket burst of hardened steel
A charming light on this fair place
These technicians' tricks appeal
Mixing with courage a little grace

Two star shells first
In rose pink burst
Two breasts you lay bare with a laugh
Offer their insolent tips
    HERE LIES
ONE WHO COULD LOVE
    some epitaph

A poet in the forest sees
Indifferent able to cope
His revolver catch at safe
Roses dying of their hope

Thinks of Saadi's roses then
Bows his head draws down his lip
As a rose reminds him of
The softer curving of a hip

The air is full of a terrible
Liquor from half-shut stars distilled
Projectiles stroke the soft nocturnal
Perfume with your image filled
Where the roses all are killed

Guillaume Apollinaire
Trans. Oliver Bernard

Herbert Read.

THE DUG-OUT

Why do you lie with your legs ungainly huddled,
And one arm bent across your sullen cold
Exhausted face? It hurts my heart to watch you,
Deep-shadow'd from the candle's guttering gold:
And you wonder why I shake you by the shoulder;
Drowsy, you mumble and sigh and shift your head . . .
You are too young to fall asleep for ever;
And when you sleep you remind me of the dead.

Siegfried Sassoon

"Why do you lie with your
legs ungainly huddled, . . ."

NIGHT ON THE CONVOY
(Alexandria-Marseilles)

Out in the blustering darkness, on the deck
A gleam of stars looks down. Long blurs of black,
The lean Destroyers, level with our track,
Plunging and stealing, watch the perilous way
Through backward racing seas and caverns of chill spray.

One sentry by the davits, in the gloom
Stands mute; the boat heaves onward through the night.
Shrouded is every chink of cabined light:
And sluiced by floundering waves that hiss and boom
And crash like guns, the troop-ship shudders . . . doom.

Now something at my feet stirs with a sigh;
And slowly growing used to groping dark,
I know that the hurricane-deck, down all its length,
Is heaped and spread with lads in sprawling strength,—
Blanketed soldiers sleeping. In the stark
Danger of life at war, they lie so still,
All prostrate and defenceless, head by head . . .
And I remember Arras, and that hill
Where dumb with pain I stumbled among the dead.

We are going home. The troop-ship, in a thrill
Of fiery-chamber'd anguish, throbs and rolls.
We are going home . . . victims . . . three thousand souls.

Siegfried Sassoon

THE NEXT WAR

The long war had ended.
Its miseries had grown faded.
Deaf men became difficult to talk to,
Heroes became bores.
Those alchemists
Who had converted blood into gold
Had grown elderly.
But they held a meeting,
Saying,
"We think perhaps we ought
To put up tombs
Or erect altars
To those brave lads
Who were so willingly burnt,
Or blinded,
Or maimed,
Who lost all likeness to a living thing,
Or were blown to bleeding patches of flesh
For our sakes.
It would look well.
Or we might even educate the children."
But the richest of these wizards
Coughed gently;

And he said:
   "I have always been to the front
   —In private enterprise—,
   I yield in public spirit
   To no man.
   I think yours is a very good idea
   —A capital idea—
   And not too costly . . .
   But it seems to me
   That the cause for which we fought
   Is again endangered.
   What more fitting memorial for the fallen
   Than that their children
   Should fall for the same cause?"
Rushing eagerly into the street,
The kindly old gentlemen cried
To the young:
   "Will you sacrifice
   Through your lethargy
   What your fathers died to gain?
   The world *must* be made safe for the young!"
And the children
Went . . .

Osbert Sitwell

HUMILITY

I know. It is not easy to explain
Why should there be such agony to bear?
Why should the whole wide world be full of pain?
But then, why should her hair
Be like the sudden sunshine after rain?

Turn cynic if you will. Curse God and die.
You've ample reason for it. There's enough
Of bitterness, God knows, to answer why.
The road of life is rough,
But then there is the glory of the sky.

I find it ever thus. I scorn the sun.
I con the book of years in bitter rage.
I swear that faith in God is dead and done,
But then I turn a page,
And shake my sides with laughter at His fun.

If life were only tragedy all through,
And I could play some high heroic part,
With fate and evil furies to pursue,
I would with steadfast heart,
But my fine tragic parts are never true.

God always laughs and spoils them, and for me
He sets the stage to suit a human fool,
Who blunders in where angels fear to be,
So if life is His School,
I trow He means to teach Humility.

Revd. G. A. Studdert Kennedy

1919

"The Treaty was all a great pity. We shall have to do the same thing all over again in 25 years at three times the cost."

**Lloyd George, to Sir William Wiseman, quoted in
Arthur Walworth's** *Woodrow Wilson—World Prophet*

On his arrival in Europe, Woodrow Wilson was greeted as the Saviour of World Peace and he was determined to justify this title when the Versailles Conference opened on 18th January 1919. Delegates from 27 victorious nations assembled to redraw the map of the world and usher in an era of universal peace with the creation of the League of Nations. The Great War, it seemed, was to be the "war to end war" as Wilson had proclaimed.

Troops were demobilized in stages. Siegfried Sassoon remained on indefinite sick leave, and on 12th March 1919 was placed on the retired list on account of ill-health caused by wounds. He left the army with the rank of captain.

Ivor Gurney had shown very serious signs of mental instability since 1918. He wrote frequently of suicide and in October of that year was discharged from the army. He attempted to take up his musical studies again and had a variety of jobs—church organist, farm worker, tax clerk, cinema pianist. In September 1922 he was committed to Barnwood House, a private asylum in Gloucester, after going to the police station every morning to request a gun so that he might shoot himself. He passed into intermittent insanity until his death in 1937. He was not always aware that the Great War had ended, and consequently went on writing "war poetry" about a war that had ceased. Edmund Blunden championed Gurney's poetry and at the time of his death in 1937 he was beginning to be recognised as a composer of some distinction.

Near the end of the war Edmund Blunden was sent on training leave. He found it impossible to resettle in academic life at Oxford after the war and went into journalism. He became Professor of English at Tokyo University, and from 1953 was Head of the English Department at the University in Hong Kong. In 1967 he was elected Oxford Professor of Poetry. Graves was unsettled by the war and by marital problems. He, too, failed to accommodate himself to the rigours of university study after the war, but was permitted to submit his critical work, *Unreason and Other Studies*, for his B.Litt., and finally graduated in 1925. For a short time he was Professor of English at Cairo and then, having finally parted from his wife, Nancy Nicholson, he went to Deya, Majorca, with

German cartoon of Greed, Revenge and other devils
drawing up the Treaty of Versailles.

the American poet Laura Riding. Graves' literary output was prolific—criticism, novels, poetry—but he suppressed his war poetry when assembling his poetry for the collected edition. He was Oxford Professor of Poetry in 1961, and in 1968 he was awarded the Queen's Gold Medal for Poetry.

For those who experienced it, the war remained an overwhelming influence. In a way there is not a great deal of difference between Gurney, who thought the war was still going on, and those to whom it was still so vivid that they continued to write about it. Herbert Read published some of his finest work about the war after 1918. Blunden, Graves and Sassoon all published accounts of their war experiences a decade after the Armistice. 1929 saw the publication of two outstanding novels about the war (Erich Maria Remarque's *All Quiet on the Western Front* and Ernest Hemingway's *A Farewell to Arms*), one of the most influential memoirs (Robert Graves' *Goodbye to All That*), and the production of one of the most significant dramas of the war (R.C. Sherriff's *Journey's End*), it seems something of an *annus mirabilis*.

Interest in the war from an historical, social and psychological point of view has never waned. Professor Paul Fussell has ably demonstrated, in *The Great War and Modern Memory*, how British experience on the

*In January 1919, Punch depicted
the figure of 'Peace' listening outside the
Allied Conference Chamber, saying: "I know
I shall have to wait for a while; but I
do hope they won't talk too much."*

Western Front has been remembered, conventionalized and mytholo-gized by various literary means. The war endured, and continues to endure in the public imagination, in the processes of cultural produc-tion, distribution and reproduction, from one generation to the next. These supplement personal memories which will come to an end once the generation who actually lived through the 1914–18 war has passed on. It seems that as we move over the years from books to plays, through film to the age of television, each age will receive images and impressions of the war which are different, and different in ways which are interestingly shaped, textured and conditioned by the means of cultural production.

It still impresses me that so many people are first moved to an interest in the Great War through coming across the "war poets"—often at school. Many people learn from their reading of Owen, Sassoon, Rosenberg, Graves and the others something of the huge impact of words and images on the imagination, and—maybe for the first time—sense the power of what poetry can do. This is to continue to pay allegiance to the art which we believe began with Homer 700 years before the birth of Christ. Homer still remains the greatest war poet but we must number several of the poets of 1914–18 his worthy descendants.

WAR BOOKS

"What did they expect of our toil and extreme
Hunger—the perfect drawing of a heart's dream?
Did they look for a book of wrought art's perfection,
Who promised no reading, nor praise, nor publication?
Out of the heart's sickness the spirit wrote
For delight, or to escape hunger, or of war's worst anger,
When the guns died to silence and men would gather sense
Somehow together, and find this was life indeed,
And praise another's nobleness, or to Cotswold get hence.
There we wrote—Corbie Ridge—or in Gonnehem at rest.
Or Fauquissart or world's death songs, ever the best.
One made sorrows' praise passing the Church where silence
Opened for the long quivering strokes of the bell—
Another wrote all soldiers' praise, and of France and night's stars.
Served his guns, got immortality, and died well.
But Ypres played another trick with its danger on me,
Kept still the needing and loving of action body;
Gave no candles, and nearly killed me twice as well,
And no souvenirs though I risked my life in the stuck tanks,
Yet there was praise of Ypres, love came sweet in hospital
And old Flanders went under to long ages of plays thought in my pages."

Ivor Gurney

Victory celebrations in London; the American contingent parades.

TO THE UNKNOWN WARRIOR

You whom the kings saluted; who refused not
    The one great pleasure of ignoble days,
Fame without name and glory without gossip,
    Whom no biographer befouls with praise.

Who said of you "Defeated"? In the darkness
    The dug-out where the limelight never comes,
Nor the big drum of Barnum's show can shatter
    That vibrant stillness after all the drums.

Though the time comes when every Yankee circus
    Can use our soldiers for its sandwich-men,
When those that pay the piper call the tune,
    You will not dance. You will not move again.

You will not march for Fatty Arbuckle,
    Though he have yet a favourable press,
Tender as San Francisco to St. Francis
    Or all the angels of Los Angeles.

They shall not storm the last unfallen fortress,
    The lonely castle where uncowed and free,
Dwells the unknown and undefeated warrior
    That did alone defeat Publicity.

Gilbert Keith Chesterton

RECALLING WAR

Entrance and exit wounds are silvered clean,
The track aches only when the rain reminds.
The one-legged man forgets his leg of wood,
The one-armed man his jointed wooden arm.
The blinded man sees with his ears and hands
As much or more than once with both his eyes.
Their war was fought these twenty years ago
And now assumes the nature-look of time,
As when the morning traveller turns and views
His wild night-stumbling carved into a hill.

What, then, was war? No mere discord of flags
But an infection of the common sky
That sagged ominously upon the earth
Even when the season was the airiest May.
Down pressed the sky, and we, oppressed, thrust out
Boastful tongue, clenched fist and valiant yard.
Natural infirmities were out of mode,
For Death was young again: patron alone
Of healthy dying, premature fate-spasm.

Fear made fine bed-fellows. Sick with delight
At life's discovered transitoriness,
Our youth became all-flesh and waived the mind.
Never was such antiqueness of romance,
Such tasty honey oozing from the heart.
And old importances came swimming back—
Wine, meat, log-fires, a roof over the head,
A weapon at the thigh, surgeons at call.
Even there was a use again for God—
A word of rage in lack of meat, wine, fire,
In ache of wounds beyond all surgeoning.

War was return of earth to ugly earth,
War was foundering of sublimities,
Extinction of each happy art and faith
By which the world had still kept head in air.
Protesting logic or protesting love,
Until the unendurable moment struck—
The inward scream, the duty to run mad.

And we recall the merry ways of guns—
Nibbling the walls of factory and church
Like a child, piecrust; felling groves of trees
Like a child, dandelions with a switch!
Machine-guns rattle toy-like from a hill,
Down in a row the brave tin-soldiers fall:
A sight to be recalled in elder days
When learnedly the future we devote
To yet more boastful visions of despair.

Robert Graves

*"Lorries a mile away, creeping along the green and yellow
ridges of the June landscape like large insects . . ."*

"Shaken from sleep, and numbed and scarce awake,
Out in the trench with three hours' watch to take, . . ."

THE CENOTAPH
September 1919

Not yet will those measureless fields be green again
Where only yesterday the wild sweet blood of wonderful youth
    was shed;
There is a grave whose earth must hold too long, too deep a stain,
Though for ever over it we may speak as proudly as we may
    tread.
But here, where the watchers by lonely hearths from the thrust of
    an inward sword have more slowly bled,
We shall build the Cenotaph: Victory, winged, with Peace,
    winged too, at the column's head.
And over the stairway, at the foot—oh! here, leave desolate,
    passionate hands to spread
Violets, roses, and laurel, with the small, sweet, twinkling
    country things
Speaking so wistfully of other Springs,
From the little gardens of little places where son or sweetheart
    was born and bred.
In splendid sleep, with a thousand brothers
    To lovers—to mothers
    Here, too, lies he:
Under the purple, the green, the red,
It is all young life: it must break some women's hearts to see
Such a brave, gay coverlet to such a bed!
Only, when all is done and said,
God is not mocked and neither are the dead.
For this will stand in our Market-place—
    Who'll sell, who'll buy
    (Will you or I
Lie each to each with the better grace)?
While looking into every busy whore's and huckster's face
As they drive their bargains, is the Face
Of God: and some young, piteous, murdered face.

Charlotte Mew

Rudyard Kipling.

SALONIKAN GRAVE

I have watched a thousand days
Pushed out and crawl into night
Slowly as tortoises.
Now I, too, follow these.
It is fever, and not the fight—
Time, not battle,—that slays.

Rudyard Kipling

THE BRIDEGROOM

Call me not false, beloved,
    If, from thy scarce-known breast
So little time removed,
    In other arms I rest.

For this more ancient bride,
    Whom coldly I embrace,
Was constant at my side
    Before I saw thy face.

Our marriage, often set—
    By miracle delayed—
At last is consummate,
    And cannot be unmade.

Live, then, whom life shall cure,
    Almost, of memory,
And leave us to endure
    Its immortality.

Rudyard Kipling

SMILE, SMILE, SMILE

Head to limp head, the sunk-eyed wounded scanned
Yesterday's *Mail*; the casualties (typed small)
And (large) Vast Booty from our Latest Haul.
Also, they read of Cheap Homes, not yet planned,
"For", said the paper, "when this war is done
The men's first instincts will be making homes.
Meanwhile their foremost need is aerodromes,
It being certain war has but begun.
Peace would do wrong to our undying dead,—
The sons we offered might regret they died
If we got nothing lasting in their stead.
We must be solidly indemnified.
Though all be worthy Victory which all bought,
We rulers sitting in this ancient spot
Would wrong our very selves if we forgot
The greatest glory will be theirs who fought,
Who kept this nation in integrity."
Nation?—The half-limbed readers did not chafe
But smiled at one another curiously
Like secret men who know their secret safe.
(This is the thing they know and never speak,
That England one by one had fled to France,
Not many elsewhere now, save under France.)
Pictures of these broad smiles appear each week,
And people in whose voice real feeling rings
Say: How they smile! They're happy now, poor things.

Wilfred Owen

THE NEXT WAR

Out there, we walked quite friendly up to Death,—
    Sat down and ate beside him, cool and bland,—
    Pardoned his spilling mess tins in our hand.
We've sniffed the green thick odour of his breath,—
Our eyes wept, but our courage didn't writhe.
    He's spat at us with bullets, and he's coughed
    Shrapnel. We chorused if he sang aloft,
We whistled while he shaved us with his scythe.

Oh, Death was never enemy of ours!
    We laughed at him, we leagued with him, old chum.
No soldier's paid to kick against His powers.
    We laughed,—knowing that better men would come,
And greater wars: when every fighter brags
He fights on Death, for lives; not men, for flags.

Wilfred Owen

Wilfred Owen.

FUTILITY

Move him into the sun—
Gently its touch awoke him once,
At home, whispering of fields half-sown.
Always it woke him, even in France,
Until this morning and this snow.
If anything might rouse him now
The kind old sun will know.

Think how it wakes the seeds—
Woke once the clays of a cold star.
Are limbs, so dear achieved, are sides
Full-nerved, still warm, too hard to stir?
Was it for this the clay grew tall?
—O what made fatuous sunbeams toil
To break earth's sleep at all?

Wilfred Owen

STRANGE MEETING

It seemed that out of battle I escaped
Down some profound dull tunnel, long since scooped
Through granites which titanic wars had groined.

Yet also there encumbered sleepers groaned,
Too fast in thought or death to be bestirred.
Then, as I probed them, one sprang up, and stared
With piteous recognition in fixed eyes,
Lifting distressful hands, as if to bless.
And by his smile, I knew that sullen hall,—
By his dead smile I knew we stood in Hell.

With a thousand pains that vision's face was grained;
Yet no blood reached there from the upper ground,
And no guns thumped, or down the flues made moan.
"Strange friend," I said, "here is no cause to mourn."
"None," said that other, "save the undone years,
The hopelessness. Whatever hope is yours,
Was my life also; I went hunting wild
After the wildest beauty in the world,
Which lies not calm in eyes, or braided hair,
But mocks the steady running of the hour,
And if it grieves, grieves richlier than here.
For by my glee might many men have laughed,
And of my weeping something had been left,
Which must die now. I mean the truth untold,
The pity of war, the pity war distilled.
Now men will go content with what we spoiled,
Or, discontent, boil bloody, and be spilled.
They will be swift with swiftness of the tigress.
None will break ranks, though nations trek from progress.
Courage was mine, and I had mystery,
Wisdom was mine, and I had mastery:
To miss the march of this retreating world
Into vain citadels that are not walled.
Then, when much blood had clogged their chariot-wheels,
I would go up and wash them from sweet wells,
Even with truths that lie too deep for taint.
I would have poured my spirit without stint
But not through wounds; not on the cess of war.
Foreheads of men have bled where no wounds were.

"I am the enemy you killed, my friend.
I knew you in this dark: for so you frowned
Yesterday through me as you jabbed and killed.
I parried; but my hands were loath and cold.
Let us sleep now . . ."

Wilfred Owen

GRASS

Pile the bodies high at Austerlitz and Waterloo.
Shovel them under and let me work.
    I am the grass; I cover all.

And pile them high at Gettysburg
And pile them high at Ypres and Verdun.
Shovel them under and let me work.

Two years, ten years, and passengers ask the conductor:
    What place is this?
    Where are we now?
    I am the grass.
    Let me work.

Carl Sandburg

A British heavy gun in action.

SONNET

On Seeing a Piece of Our Heavy Artillery
Brought into Action

Be slowly lifted up, thou long black arm,
Great Gun towering towards Heaven, about to curse;
Sway steep against them, and for years rehearse
Huge imprecations like a blasting charm!
Reach at that Arrogance which needs thy harm,
And beat it down before its sins grow worse.
Spend our resentment, cannon,—yea, disburse
Our gold in shapes of flame, our breaths in storm.

Yet, for men's sakes whom thy vast malison
Must wither innocent of enmity,
Be not withdrawn, dark arm, thy spoilure done,
Safe to the bosom of our prosperity.
But when thy spell be cast complete and whole,
May God curse thee, and cut thee from our soul!

Wilfred Owen

AFTERMATH

Have you forgotten yet? . . .
For the world's events have rumbled on since those
    gagged days,
Like traffic checked awhile at the crossing of city ways:
And the haunted gap in your mind has filled with thoughts
    that flow
Like clouds in the lit heaven of life; and you're a man
    reprieved to go,
Taking your peaceful share of Time, with joy to spare.
But the past is just the same,—and War's a bloody game . . .
Have you forgotten yet? . . .
Look down, and swear by the slain of the War that you'll
    never forget.

Do you remember the dark months you held the sector at
    Mametz,—
The nights you watched and wired and dug and piled sand-
    bags on parapets?
Do you remember the rats; and the stench
Of corpses rotting in front of the front-line trench,—
And dawn coming, dirty-white, and chill with a hopeless
    rain?
Do you ever stop and ask, "Is it all going to happen
    again?"

Do you remember that hour of din before the attack,—
And the anger, the blind compassion that seized and shook
    you then
As you peered at the doomed and haggard faces of your
    men?
Do you remember the stretcher-cases lurching back
With dying eyes and lolling heads,—those ashen-grey
Masks of the lads who once were keen and kind and
    gay?
Have you forgotten yet? . . .
Look up, and swear by the green of the Spring that you'll
    never forget.

Siegfried Sassoon

Biographies
of the
Poets

ALDINGTON, Richard (1892–1962)
Educated Dover College and University of London. Served on the Western Front 1916–18 where he was badly gassed. Married U.S. poet Hilda Doolittle. His novel *Death of a Hero* (1929), a psychological examination of a young officer killed in 1918, made him famous. Also numbered among his achievements are his *Collected Poems* (1929), controversial biographies of Wellington, T.E. Lawrence, and D.H. Lawrence, and *Life for Life's Sake* (1940)—his autobiography. He was a leading exponent of the Imagist school which included Pound, Ford Madox Ford, Amy Lowell and Hilda Doolittle. Died in the south of France.

APOLLINAIRE, Guillaume (1880–1918)
The poet's real name was Wilhelm Apollinaris Kostrowitzky. He was the illegitimate son of an aristocratic Polish mother and an Italian father. Educated at schools on the Riviera, he began life as a tutor in Germany and then went to Paris where he worked in a bank, taking part in literary and artistic life. He was a friend of Picasso, Dufy, Modigliani and other Cubists and Futurists. When he joined the French army in 1914 he thought war was a great adventure and was an exemplary soldier. In 1916 he was badly wounded in the head and never really recovered. He died in the influenza epidemic of 1918. His major collections of poetry are *Alcools* (1913) and *Calligrammes* (1918).

ASQUITH, Herbert (1881–1947)
Son of the Prime Minister. Educated Winchester, and Balliol. President of the Oxford Union. Served as a captain in the Royal Artillery. Published works include *The Volunteer and Other Poems*, and *Poems 1912–33*. His brother Arthur was a close friend of Rupert Brooke. Another brother, Raymond, wrote light verse, and was killed serving as a lieutenant in the Grenadier Guards at the Somme 1916.

BARBUSSE, Henri (1874–1935)
Before the war, Barbusse was a journalist. He volunteered for military service and was an exemplary soldier, but became disillusioned with the war. His influential novel *Le Feu* (1916) was awarded the Prix Goncourt and was widely read in its English translation by F. Wray. As a Marxist, his views became more politically focused and his work more didactic. He published work on Lenin and Stalin, and died in Moscow.

BARING, Maurice (1874–1945)
Educated Eton, and Cambridge. He was a diplomat and foreign correspondent for *Morning Post* and *The Times*, and served in the Royal Flying Corps. Baring published five novels, his *Collected Poems* (1925), and his autobiography. He also wrote plays, and was a friend of Edward Marsh.

BINYON, Laurence (1869–1943)
Educated St. Paul's School, and Trinity College, Oxford. Before going to the Front, Binyon was on the staff of the British Museum where he became an authority on Chinese and Japanese art. He published work on Botticelli, Blake and English water colourists, and also his *Collected Poems* (1931). He is best known for his poem *For the Fallen* (1914).

BISHOP, John Peale (1892–1944)
Educated Princeton. Served with U.S. 33rd Infantry in France. Bishop was a friend of F. Scott Fitzgerald and was the original of Tom D'Invilliers in Fitzgerald's *This Side of Paradise* (1920). Published works include his novel *Act of Darkness* (1935), *Collected Essays* (1948), *Collected Poems* (1948), and *Selected Essays* (1960).

BLUNDEN, Edmund (1896–1974)
Educated Christ's Hospital, and The Queen's College. Blunden served with the Royal Sussex Regiment 1915–19, was at the Somme and Ypres, and was awarded the Military Cross. *Undertones of War* (1928) is a brilliant account of his war experiences. He held academic posts in Tokyo and Hong Kong, was a fellow of Merton College, Oxford 1931–44, and Oxford Professor of Poetry 1967–68. He published studies of Lamb, Hunt, Shelley, and Hardy, encouraged a revival of interest in John Clare, and also edited important editions of Owen and Gurney. He was a friend of Siegfried Sassoon.

BRITTAIN, Vera (1896–1970)
Born in Newcastle-under-Lyme and educated at Somerville College, Oxford, after which she left to work as a Voluntary Aid Nurse during the war. Her autobiographical account of this period, *Testament of Youth*, is a masterpiece. After the war she went back to Oxford. She married Professor George E.G. Catlin of Cornell University. Shirley Williams, the politician, is their daughter.

BROOKE, Rupert (1887–1915)
Born and educated at Rugby, where his father was a master, and at King's College, Cambridge. Brooke was a precocious boy and brilliant undergraduate. He was a founder member of the Marlowe Society and a Fabian. Brooke's first volume of poems was published in 1911. A protégé of Edward Marsh, he became a fellow of King's College, and produced interesting work on Jacobean drama. Brooke mixed in glittering literary society—Masefield, Gibson, Abercrombie, Drinkwater, the Asquith boys were all friends. He saw action at Antwerp and died of blood poisoning while serving with the Royal Naval Division in the Dardanelles campaign. His *Collected Poems* (1918) included the famous '1914' group of sonnets which were first published in 1915.

CANNAN, May Wedderburn (1893–1973)
Born in Oxford, educated at Wychwood School, May Wedderburn Cannan worked as a nurse and in the Intelligence Service during the war. She later worked for the Oxford University Press and was a librarian at the Athenaeum Club in London.

CHESTERTON, Gilbert Keith (1874–1936)
Educated St. Paul's School, and the Slade, and made a reputation as a prolific journalist for papers such as *The Bookman*, *Daily News*, and *Illustrated London News*. He was a master of paradox with the ability seemingly to write about anything on earth. He wrote several entertaining novels and a lot of light verse, as well as several critical volumes—on Browning, Shaw, Thackeray and Dickens.

COLE, Margaret Postgate (1893–1980)
Educated Roedean, and Girton College, Cambridge, she devoted her life to politics. She worked in the Fabian Research Department, wrote books in collaboration with her husband (G.D.H. Cole), and also wrote detective novels. She worked tirelessly for the London County Council.

COULSON, Leslie (1889–1916)
Before 1914 was a well-known Fleet Street journalist. He served in the Royal Fusiliers from September 1914 and was wounded at Gallipoli. He served as a sergeant at the Somme in 1916 where he was killed, aged 27. *From an Outpost and Other Poems* (1917) was a best seller.

DE LA MARE, Walter (1873–1956)
Educated St. Paul's Cathedral Choristers' School. Until 1908 he worked for the Anglo-American Oil Company. He published a collection of poetry—*Songs of Childhood* (1902)—followed by novels, stories, children's books and several brilliant anthologies. His poetry is strangely compelling and otherworldly, yet tough and often bizarre.

EHRENSTEIN, Albert (1886–1950)
Born in Vienna. Ehrenstein was an Expressionist poet who first achieved celebrity in Karl Krauss' journal *Fackel*. He was a friend of Oskar Kokoschka, who illustrated several of his works. Much of his poetry is socio-political. He travelled widely in Africa and Asia, emigrated from Austria in 1932, and died in New York.

FORD, Ford Madox (1873–1939)
Educated University College School, London. He was the son of a distinguished music critic, his grandfather was Ford Madox Brown, the painter, and his aunt married William Rossetti. He published poetry and two novels in collaboration with Conrad. Ford served in a Welsh infantry regiment and was gassed. After the war he published a series of war novels, some poetry, and several volumes of autobiography.

FREEMAN, John (1880–1929)
Freeman left school at the age of 12 and became a clerk in an insurance company. He was director of the company by 1927. He published numerous volumes of verse, including *Poems New and Old* (1920) for which he won the Hawthornden Prize,

and also some journalism and literary criticism: *George Moore* (1922), and *Herman Melville* (1926).

GIBSON Wilfrid Wilson (1878–1962)
A close friend of Rupert Brooke and protégé of Edward Marsh, Gibson worked as a social worker in the East End of London. His earliest published poetry was *Mountain Lovers* (1902), and several important poems in various volumes of *Georgian Poetry*. He was interested in portraying working and agricultural life, as in *Daily Bread* (1910). Served in the ranks from 1914 but was only briefly at the Front. His *Collected Poems 1905–25* were published in 1926.

GRAVES, Robert von Ranke (1895–1985)
Graves had a literary and academic background. His mother was German. He was educated at Charterhouse, and went straight into the Royal Welch Fusiliers at the beginning of the war. He was friends with Owen, Sassoon and Nichols. Much of his early war poetry he later suppressed from collected editions of his verse. The success of his autobiography *Goodbye to All That* (1929) enabled him to become a full time writer; he became a poet, novelist, critic and scholar. He was awarded a B.Litt. at Oxford after the war, he taught for a time in Cairo, and then went to live in Majorca. He was Professor of Poetry at Oxford 1961–6.

GRENFELL, Julian (1888–1915)
Son of Lord Desborough, educated at Eton and Balliol. As a regular officer in 1910 he served in the Royal Dragoons. He was mentioned in Dispatches twice, and was awarded the Distinguished Service Order. His poem *Into Battle* is one of the most anthologized poems of modern times. He died of wounds, aged 27, on 30th April 1915.

GURNEY, Ivor (1890–1937)
Born in Gloucester, the son of a tailor. Gurney was educated at King's School, Gloucester as a chorister and he won an Open Scholarship to the Royal College of Music where he was a student of Sir Charles Stanford. He wrote music and poetry from an early stage, and was always highly sensitive and moody. Gurney volunteered for the Gloucester regiment, he was initially turned down because of his poor eyesight but finally joined in 1915. He served in France, was wounded and gassed and sent home. His poems *Severn and Somme* (1917) went into a 2nd edition, and while employed in a variety of jobs he wrote a lot of music. By 1918 signs of serious mental disturbance had appeared, and in 1922 he was committed to an asylum in Gloucester and was later transferred to Dartford. After this he never left hospital and believed at times the war still continued. He died in 1937.

HARDY, Thomas (1840–1928)
Born at Higher Bockhampton, near Dorchester. Educated at a private school in Dorchester where from 1856 he went on to study church architecture. He was acquainted with William Barnes, the poet and linguist—the dialect poet of Dorset—and studied Latin and Greek. He received creative literary criticism and advice from George Meredith. Between 1871 and 1895 Hardy published a remarkable series of novels, but the hostile critical reaction to *Jude the Obscure* led him to turn to poetry

again. A period of outstanding lyrical achievement followed: *Wessex Poems* (1898), *Poems of Past and Present* (1901), *Time's Laughing Stock* (1909). His dramatic epic on the Napoleonic wars *The Dynasts* occupied him between 1903–08.

HARVEY, F.W. (1888–?)

Born in Gloucestershire, a childhood friend of Ivor Gurney. In adult life he worked as a solicitor. As a lance corporal in the Gloucestershire Regiment, he won the Distinguished Conduct Medal and was later commissioned. In 1916 he was taken prisoner. His poetry was allowed to be sent to London from prison camp by the German authorities. *Gloucestershire Friends* (1917), and *Comrades in Captivity* (1919) are collections of his verse.

HEYM, Georg (1887–1912)

Born in Hirschberg, Silesia. Heym was influenced by Baudelaire and Rimbaud. He was one of the earliest Expressionists. *Der Ewige Tag* (1911) and *Umbra Vitae* (1912) suggest he had a foreboding of the terrible events of 1914–18.

HODGSON, W.N. (1893–1916)

Educated Durham School, and Christ Church, Oxford. He was influenced by Rupert Brooke. Hodgson volunteered in 1914 and served in the Devonshire Regiment. He was mentioned in Dispatches, and was awarded the Military Cross in 1915. His excellent short stories and poetry were published in *The Spectator*, and *Saturday Post*. He was killed on the first day of the Somme, 1st July 1916. His *Verse and Prose in War and Peace* was published in 1917.

HOUSMAN, Alfred Edward (1859–1936)

Educated Bromsgrove School, and St. John's College, Oxford. For a while Housman worked in the Patent Office, but his reputation for being a meticulous and erudite classical scholar soon earned him the professorship of Latin and Greek at University College, London. He later became a professor at Cambridge. He produced outstanding work on Propertius, Manilius, and was a master of scathing critical prose. As well as *A Shropshire Lad* (1896), for which he is widely known, Housman also wrote *Last Poems* (1922) and *More Poems* (1936).

JONES, David (1895–1974)

Born in Kent. Jones studied Art before serving with the Royal Welch Fusiliers 1915–18. W.H. Auden described Jones' *In Parenthesis* (1937) not as "a war book so much as a distillation of the essence of war books". It won the Hawthornden Prize in 1938. He became a leading painter of the time and his work was exhibited by the Tate Gallery and the Victoria and Albert Museum. In 1955 he was made a Commander of the British Empire.

KETTLE, T.M. (1880–1916)

Son of a famous Irish land reformer. Kettle was a lawyer, M.P. for North-East Tyrone 1906–10, and then professor of National Economics at University College, Dublin. He was an essayist, journalist and poet; he joined the Dublin Fusiliers early in the war, and was killed at the Somme, 8th September 1916.

KIPLING, Rudyard (1865–1936)

Born in Bombay. Educated United Services College, Westward Ho! in Devon. He worked as a journalist in Lahore, returning to London in 1889. He married an American and lived for four years in Vermont, returning to England in 1896. Kipling produced a vast quantity of prose and verse of considerable diversity. His children's books—*The Jungle Book*, *Puck of Pook's Hill*, and *Just So Stories* have become classics. His son was killed in the First World War serving with the Irish Guards. In 1923 he published *The Irish Guards in the Great War*. He declined the Poet Laureateship and the Order of Merit (the latter three times), but was awarded a Nobel Prize in 1907.

LETTS, Winifred M. (1882–1971)

Born in Ireland, educated in Bromley. She served as a Voluntary Aid Detachment nurse from 1915, and worked in Manchester and Alnwick.

LICHTENSTEIN, Alfred (1881–1914)

Born in Berlin. Lichtenstein was an Expressionist who, as well as writing poetry, wrote books for children. He was killed in action near Reims in 1914. His collected verse was published posthumously: *Gedichte* (1929), and *Gesammelte Gedichte*, (1962).

MACAULAY, Dame Rose (1881–1958)

Born in Cambridge, educated Oxford High School and Somerville College, Oxford. Despite spending much of her life in Italy, Macaulay was a member of the Bloomsbury group. She published over 20 novels, and also wrote fine critical studies of Milton and E.M. Forster.

McCRAE, John (1872–1918)

John McCrae is famous for one striking poem: *In Flanders Fields*. McCrae was a Canadian physician who began to write poetry while a student at McGill University. He made considerable contributions to pathology. He began his military career in the artillery on the Western Front in 1914, but was transferred to the medical service and was put in charge of a hospital in Boulogne. Early in 1918 he was appointed consultant in charge of the British Armies in France, but died of pneumonia before he could take up his duties. *In Flanders Fields and Other Poems* was published in 1919.

MASEFIELD, John (1878–1967)

Born in Ledbury, Herefordshire. As a young man he served as a seaman, and worked in America. Influenced by Kipling and Conrad, he wrote long, often romantic, narrative poems and imaginative fiction for younger readers. He was appointed Poet Laureate in 1930, and was awarded the Order of Merit in 1935.

MASTIN, Florence Ripley (1896–)

Educated Columbia University, she subsequently taught English at a high school in Brooklyn. She has won several poetry awards, and has contributed to *Saturday Review* and *New York Times*.

MEW, Charlotte (1869–1928)

Born in Bloomsbury, educated at Lucy Harrison School for Girls. She suffered from ill-health, family bereavements, and poverty. Mew was rather an eccentric, and was often to be seen at the Poetry Bookshop in Bloomsbury in male attire. Her poetry was recognized by Hardy, Masefield and de la Mare and she was awarded a Civil List pension. She committed suicide.

MEYNELL, Alice (1847–1922)
Born in Barnes, she spent her childhood in Italy. Meynell was a poet and essayist. Browning, Tennyson, Rossetti, Patmore, George Eliot, and Ruskin were all friends and associates. In 1877 she married Wilfred Meynell, biographer and journalist.

NEWBOLT, Sir Henry (1862–1938)
Educated Clifton College (a contemporary of Douglas Haig), and Corpus Christi College, Oxford. He practised as a barrister 1887–99. Newbolt published some rather jingoistic poetry such as *Drake's Drum* (1896), as well as finely wrought but typically late-Victorian romantic and sentimental verse. Some of his work, such as *The Vigil*, written for previous wars, was given new life by the spirit of 1914. He also wrote fiction, criticism, and two volumes of the official naval history 1914–18. He was knighted in 1915 and awarded the Companion of Honour in 1922.

NICHOLS, Robert (1893–1944)
Educated Winchester, and Trinity College, Oxford. He served with the Royal Artillery 1914–16, and fought at the Somme. A protégé of Edward Marsh and a member of the Georgian group, Nichols was a close friend of Brooke and Sassoon. After only three weeks in France, he was invalided home with shell shock in 1916 and subsequently worked for the Ministry of Information. Despite his not having been involved in any "show" at the Front, he became a famous "soldier poet" with *Invocation: War Poems* (1915), and *Ardours and Endurances* (1917).

OWEN, Wilfred (1893–1918)
Born in Oswestry, educated at Birkenhead Institute, and University of London. Owen was tutor to a family in Bordeaux 1913–15 before enlisting with the Artists' Rifles. While recovering from shell shock at Craiglockhart Hospital near Edinburgh, he met Sassoon and Graves. Ironically, Owen was killed only a week before the Armistice. His *Poems*, collected by Sassoon, are among the most poignant of the war.

POPE, Jessie (?–1941)
Educated North London Collegiate School. Pope was a regular contributor to *Punch* and other journals.

READ, Sir Herbert (1893–1968)
Born in Kirbymoorside, Yorkshire, and educated at Leeds University. During the war he was a captain in the Yorkshire Regiment, and was awarded the Distinguished Service Order and Military Cross. After the war he worked in the Treasury, and became Assistant Keeper at the Victoria and Albert Museum. As well as several volumes of poetry, he published literary and fine art criticism.

RICKWORD, Edgell (1898–1982)
Rickword served in the infantry on the Western Front. He published many poems in various war time journals, and

Behind the Eyes (1921) contains some of his best war poems. Politically a radical, he was also an invigorating literary critic and an associate of F.R. Leavis.

ROSENBERG, Isaac (1890–1918)
Born in Bristol, educated at Stepney, and the Slade. He had work exhibited at the Whitechapel Gallery. Rosenberg enlisted in the Lancaster Regiment, and was killed in action on the Western Front 1st April 1918. His war poetry is an early example of Modernism.

SACKVILLE, Margaret (1881–1963)
Daughter of the 7th Earl de la Warr, Lady Sackville was a poet and children's author. She lived her early life in Edinburgh, and died in Cheltenham.

SANDBURG, Carl (1878–1967)
Born in Illinois, Sandburg travelled a lot in early life. He served in Puerto Rico during the American War, studied at Lombard College on his return, and then worked in journalism in Chicago. He published several important volumes of poetry over a period of 20 years. He also published an imaginative biography of Lincoln, and an outstanding account of his early life.

SASSOON, Siegfried (1886–1967)
Born in Kent, educated Marlborough, and Clare College, Cambridge. Before the war, Sassoon enjoyed the life of a country gentleman and literary dilettante. He enlisted in 1914 and served as lieutenant in the Royal Welch Fusiliers, where he met Robert Graves. At Craiglockhart Hospital he met Wilfred Owen. An exceptionally courageous regimental officer, as the war dragged on he developed strong pacifist sentiments and in 1917, encouraged by Bertrand Russell, he made an official protest against the war's continuation. Sassoon's war poetry and fictionalized autobiography rank among the finest writings on the Great War.

SCHNACK, Anton (1892–   )
Schnack was born in Rieneck, Franconia and was the brother of the German novelist Friedrich Schnack. His experiences in the German army 1914–18 formed the inspiration for his first major collection of poetry: *Tier rang gewaltig mit Tier* (1920). He has published several volumes of poetry since then, and this later work is more lyrical.

SEEGER, Alan (1888–1916)
Born in New York, educated Harvard. Seeger served in the French Foreign Legion 1914–16, and was killed during the first few days of the Somme. His *Collected Poems* were published in 1916, the poem *Rendezvous* made him famous.

SINCLAIR, May (1865–1946)
Educated Cheltenham Ladies College. Sinclair served with the Red Cross in the Field Ambulance Corps. She wrote short stories and novels and was influenced by the ideas of Freud.

SITWELL, Dame Edith (1887–1964)
Sitwell was the daughter of Sir George Sitwell, and sister of Osbert and Sacheverell. She was a prolific writer, a formative

influence in contemporary poetic taste and in the revival of interest in 18th century literature. She and her brothers founded the Modernist anthology *Wheels*. She was a champion of William Walton, Wilfred Owen and Aldous Huxley, and encouraged the work of Dylan Thomas. *Clowns' Houses* (1918) was her first major poetic success.

SITWELL, Sir Osbert (1892–1969)
Educated Eton. He was the brother of Edith and Sacheverell (critic and poet). He served as an officer in the Grenadier Guards 1912–19. He wrote novels as well as poetry, and was an autobiographer of genius.

SORLEY, Charles Hamilton (1895–1915)
Born in Aberdeen, educated Marlborough and University College, Oxford. Sorley enlisted in the Suffolk Regiment in 1914, and was commissioned as captain in August 1915. He was killed at the Battle of Loos, 13th October 1915.

STADLER, Ernst (1883–1914)
Born in Colmar, he was a Rhodes Scholar and went to Magdalen College, Oxford. He held academic posts at Strasbourg, Brussels and Toronto. He joined the German army in 1914. Before the war he had worked together with René Schickele for a better understanding between France and Germany in cultural matters, his death in action at Ypres is therefore deeply ironic. *Der Aufbruch* (1914) is one of the most outstanding collections of Expressionist poetry.

STOPES, Marie Carmichael (1880–1958)
Scientist and sex reformer. Educated North London Collegiate School, and University College, London. Stopes earned her Ph.D in Munich in 1904, and D.Sc in London a year later. She was a lecturer in Palaeobotany in Manchester and London 1909–20, and was made a fellow of University College, London in 1910. She founded the Mothers' Birth Control Clinic in 1921 and was a campaigner for sex education and family planning.

STRAMM, August (1874–1915)
Stramm was born in Münster and was on the editorial board of the Expressionist journal *Der Sturm*. He was a poet and dramatist, his work has been set to music by Hindemith. He was killed in action on the Eastern Front.

STUDDERT-KENNEDY, G.A. (1883–1929)
Padre Studdert-Kennedy was well-known on the Western Front. He was nick-named "Woodbine Willie" because he always carried a pocketful of Woodbines to hand out to the troops. He wrote ballad poems in the manner of Kipling and dialect poems.

SUTHERLAND, Millicent (1867–1955)
The Duchess of Sutherland, whose vivid account of the German invasion of Belgium was published in *The Times* in 1914. She worked tirelessly for the French Red Cross and received the Croix de Guerre.

THOMAS, Edward (1878–1917)
Born in London of Welsh descent. Educated St. Paul's School, and Lincoln College, Oxford. He wrote brilliantly and evocatively of country life and countryside, was a tireless journalist and *littérateur*. He produced studies of Richard Jeffries, Swinburne, Borrow, Pater, Keats and Maeterlinck, and in later life he wrote poetry. Thomas enlisted as a private, he was a 2nd lieutenant when killed at Arras.

TRAKL, Georg (1887–1914)
Trakl was born in Salzburg and served as a lieutenant in the Medical Corps. His experiences on the Eastern Front brought on insanity and he poisoned himself at a military hospital in Crakow. He was a surrealist poet, influenced by Baudelaire and the Expressionists. His reputation rests on two outstanding volumes of poetry: *Gedichte* (1913), and *Sebastian im Traum* (1914). In his anxiety and the sense of disjointed reality in his poetry, it is possible to see the onset of his derangement.

UNGARETTI, Giuseppe (1888–1970)
Ungaretti was a poet and translator. He held academic positions in Brazil and Rome, and was a friend of Apollinaire. He volunteered for military service, and his collection of war poems *L'Allegria* was published in 1919. He continued to be a prolific writer after the war.

VERNÈDE, Robert Ernest (1875–1917)
Of French descent. Educated St. Paul's School where he was a friend of G.K. Chesterton, and St. John's College, Oxford. Vernède served with the Royal Fusiliers and was killed in action 9th April 1917. He was a novelist and poet, his *War Poems* were published in 1918 with an introduction by Edmund Gosse.

BIBLIOGRAPHY

Asquith, Herbert *Memoirs and Reflections* (Cassell, 1928)

Baily, Leslie *Scrapbook 1900–1914* (BBC, 1957)

Barbusse, Henri *Le Feu*, trans. F. Wray *Under Fire* (Dent, 1917)

Barclay, C. N. *Armistice 1918* (Dent, 1968)

Barnett, Correlli *Britain and her Army 1509–1970* (Allen Lane, 1970)

Bergonzi, Bernard *Heroes' Twilight – A Study of the Literature of the Great War* (Constable, 1965)

Blunden, Edmund *War Poets 1914–1918* (Longman, 1958)
Undertones of War (Collins, 1965)

Bold, Alan (ed.) *The Martial Muse – Seven Centuries of War Poetry* (Wheaton, Exeter, 1976)

Braddon, Russell *All the Queen's Men – The Household Cavalry and the Brigade of Guards* (Hamish Hamilton, 1977)

Brereton, J. M. *The British Soldier – A Social History 1661 to the Present Day* (Bodley Head, 1986)

Brittain, Vera *Testament of Youth* (Gollancz, 1933)

Brooke, Rupert *Collected Poems, with a Memoir by Edward Marsh* (Sidgwick and Jackson, 1930)

Brown, M. *Tommy Goes to War* (Dent, 1978)

Bullard, Robert Lee *Personalities and Reminiscences of the War* (Doubleday, NY, 1925)

Carey, G. V. and Scott, H. S. *An Outline History of the Great War* (Cambridge University Press, 1928)

Carrington, Charles *Rudyard Kipling* (Macmillan, 1978)

Churchill, Winston *The World Crisis* (Butterworth, 1923)

Cohen, Joseph *Journey to the Trenches – The Life of Isaac Rosenberg* (Robson, 1975)

Cruttwell, C. R. M. F. *A History of the Great War 1914–1918* (Paladin, 1986)

Darroch, Sandra *Ottoline* (Chatto and Windus, 1976)

David, Daniel *The 1914 Campaign* (Spellmount, Tunbridge Wells, 1987)

De La Mare, Walter *Motley and Other Poems* (Constable, 1918)

Delany, Paul *The Neo-Pagans – Friendship and Love in the Rupert Brooke Circle* (Macmillan, 1987)

Dixon, Norman F. *The Psychology of Military Incompetence* (Jonathan Cape, 1976)

Dunn, J. C. *The War the Infantry Knew 1914–1919* (Jane's, 1987)

Edel, Leon *Bloomsbury – A House of Lions* (Hogarth, 1979)

Falls, Cyril *The First World War* (Longman, 1960)
Armageddon 1918 (Weidenfeld and Nicolson, 1964)

Farrar-Hockley, A. H. *The Somme* (Pan, 1966)

Flecker, James Elroy *The Collected Poems of James Elroy Flecker* ed. J. C. Squire (Martin Secker, 1922)

Fussell, Paul *The Great War and Modern Memory* (Oxford University Press, 1975)

Gardner, Brian *Up the Line to Death – The War Poets 1914–1918* (Methuen, 1976)

Georgian Poetry 1914–1915, 1916–1917, 1918–1919 (The Poetry Bookshop)

Gibbs, Philip *Realities of War* (Heinemann, 1920)

Gilbert, Adrian *World War I in Photographs* (Orbis, 1986)

Girouard, Mark *The Return to Camelot* (Yale University Press, 1981)

Gliddon, Gerald *When the Barrage Lifts* (Gliddon Books, Norwich, 1987)

Graham, Gerald S. *A Concise History of the British Empire* (Thames and Hudson, 1972)

Graves, Richard Perceval *A. E. Housman* (Routledge and Kegan Paul, 1979)

Graves, Robert *Over the Brazier* (Poetry Bookshop, 1916)
Goliath and David (Chiswick Press, 1916)
Fairies and Fusiliers (Heinemann, 1917)
Poems 1914–1927 (Heinemann, 1927)
Goodbye to All That (Cassell, 1957)

Gurney, Ivor *Collected Poems* ed. P. J. Kavanagh (Oxford University Press, 1982)

Hardach, Gerd *The First World War 1914–1918* (Allen Lane, 1977)

Hassall, Christopher *Edward Marsh – Patron of the Arts* (Hutchinson, 1959)

Horne, Alistair *The Price of Glory – Verdun* (Macmillan, 1962)

James, Robert Rhodes *Gallipoli* (Macmillan, 1965)

Johnston, John H. *English Poetry of the First World War* (Oxford University Press, 1964)

Jones, Barbara and Howell, Bill *Popular Arts of the First World War* (Studio Vista, 1972)

Jones, David *In Parenthesis* (Faber, 1982)

Kamester, Margaret and Vellacott, Jo (eds.) *Militarism versus Feminism – Writings on Women and War* (Virago, 1987)

Keegan, John and Wheatcroft, Andrew *Who's Who in Military History* (Hutchinson, 1987)

Laffin, John *Tommy Atkins* (Cassell, 1966)
On the Western Front (Alan Sutton, 1986)

Le Bas, Hedley *The Lord Kitchener Memorial Book* (Hodder and Stoughton, 1916)

Liddell Hart, B. H. *T. E. Lawrence* (Jonathan Cape, 1934)
History of the First World War (Pan, 1970)

Liebknecht, Karl *Militarism* (Huebsch, NY, 1917)

Lloyd George, David *War Memoirs* (Nicolson and Watson, 1936)

Machen, Arthur *The Angels of Mons* (Simpkin Marshall, 1915)

Macdonald, Lyn *Somme* (Macmillan, 1983)

McGuffie, T. H. *Rank and File* (Hutchinson, 1964)

McKenzie, John M. *Propaganda and Empire* (University of Manchester Press, 1984)

Magnus, Peter *Kitchener – Portrait of an Imperialist* (Arrow, 1961)

Mangan, J.A. *Athleticism in the Victorian and Edwardian Public School* (Cambridge University Press, 1981)

Marshall-Cornwall, J. *Haig as Military Commander* (Batsford, 1973)

Marwick, Arthur *The Deluge* (Bodley Head, 1965)
War and Social Change in the Twentieth Century (Macmillan, 1974)

Maurice, Frederick *Forty Days in 1914* (Constable, 1919)

Middlebrook, Martin *The First Day of the Somme* (Penguin, 1984)

Morell, E. D. *Truth and the War* (National Labour Press, 1916)

Newbolt, Henry *Collected Poetry* (Nelson, 1908)
Tales of the Great War (Longman, 1918)

Nichols, Robert *Ardours and Endurances* (Chatto and Windus, 1917)

Owen, Wilfred *The Poems of Wilfred Owen* ed. Jon Stallworthy (Hogarth, 1985)

Parker, Peter *The Old Lie – The Great War and the Public School Ethos* (Constable, 1987)

Parsons, I. M. *Men Who March Away – Poems of the First World War* (Hogarth, 1987)

Pinto, Vivian de Sola *Crisis in English Poetry 1880–1940* (Hutchinson, 1951)

Priestley, J. B. *The Edwardians* (Heinemann, 1970)

Reeves, James (ed.) *Georgian Poetry* (Penguin, 1968)

Reilly, Catherine (ed.) *Scars Upon My Heart – Women's Poetry and Verse of the First World War* (Virago, 1981)

Rickards, Maurice and Moody, Michael *First World War Ephemera* (Jupiter, 1975)

Robbins, Keith *The First World War* (Oxford University Press, 1985)

Rosenberg, Isaac *Collected Poems* ed. Gordon Bottomley and Denys Harding (Chatto and Windus, 1974)

Ross, Robert H. *The Georgian Revolt* (Faber, 1967)

Sassoon, Siegfried *Selected Poems* (Heinemann, 1925)
Diaries 1915–1918 ed. Rupert Hart-Davis (Faber, 1983)
Memoirs of an Infantry Officer (Faber, 1985)
Sherston's Progress (Faber, 1985)

Seymour-Smith, Martin *Robert Graves – His Life and Work* (Paladin, 1987)

Silkin, Jon *Out of Battle – Poetry of the Great War* (Oxford University Press, 1972)
The Penguin Book of First World War Poetry (Allen Lane, 1978)

Sitwell, Osbert *Great Morning* (Macmillan, 1949)

Stallworthy, Jon *Wilfred Owen – A Biography* (Oxford University Press, 1974)

Strong, L. A. G. "English Poetry Since Brooke" in *Nineteenth Century*, CXVI 1934 (pp. 460–8)

Taylor, A. J. P. *The Course of German History* (Methuen, 1961)
English History 1914–1945 (Clarendon Press, 1965)

Terraine, John *Douglas Haig – The Educated Soldier* (Hutchinson, 1963)
The Western Front 1914–1918 (Hutchinson, 1964)
Mons – The Retreat to Victory (Pan, 1972)
The Smoke and the Fire – Myths and Anti-Myths of War 1861–1945 (Sidgwick and Jackson, 1980)
The First World War (Macmillan, 1984)

Thomas, Edward *Selected Poems* ed. R. S. Thomas (Faber, 1964)
A Language not to be Betrayed – Selected Prose of Edward Thomas ed. Edna Longley (Carcanet, 1981)

Travers, Tim *The Killing Ground – The British Army, the Western Front and the Emergence of Modern Warfare 1900–1918* (Allen and Unwin, 1987)

Tuchman, Barbara *August 1914* (Constable, 1962)

Turner, E. S. *Gallant Gentleman – A Portrait of the British Officer* (Michael Joseph, 1956)
Dear Old Blighty (Michael Joseph, 1980)

Vernède, Robert Ernest *War Poems and Other Verses* (Heinemann, 1917)

Watt, Richard *The Kings Depart* (Weidenfeld and Nicolson, 1969)

Williams, John *Heyday for Assassins* (Heinemann, 1958)

Winter, Denis *Death's Men – Soldiers of the Great War* (Allen Lane, 1978)

The Wipers Times – A Complete Facsimile of the Famous World War I Trench Newspaper (Peter Davies, 1973)

Woolff, Leon *In Flanders Fields* (Longman, 1959)

INDEX

Note: Bold figures refer to poems printed and italics to illustrations.
(i.) indicates the author of a painting, photograph or other illustration.

ACKNOWLEDGMENTS

The Paul Press Ltd. would like to extend their grateful thanks
to the following organizations for permission to use their material.
(Page numbers for individual pictures are in brackets.)

COLOUR ILLUSTRATIONS

The Trustees of the Imperial Museum: (18) Eric Kennington, **Back to Billets**; (35) Stanley Spencer, **Travoys Arriving with Wounded at a Dressing Station at Smol, Macedonia, September 1916**; (36) P. Wyndham Lewis, **A Battery Shelled**; (45) Joseph B. Gray, **A Ration Party of the 4th Black Watch at the Battle of Neuve Chapelle 1915**; (46) Austin O. Spare, **Operating on a Slightly Wounded Man in a Regimental Aid Post**; (47) William P. Roberts, **The Gas Chamber**; (48) Frank Dobson, **In the Trenches 1916**; (57) John Singer Sargent, **Gassed**; (58) E. Handley-Read, **Killing Germans**; (76) Colin U. Gill, **Heavy Artillery**; (77) John Singer Sargent, **The Interior of a Hospital Tent**; (95) Paul Nash, **The Menin Road**; (97) John Nash, **Oppy Wood 1917, Evening**; (98) J. Barnard Davis, **The Workroom of the Gerrard's Red Cross War Hospital Supply Depot**; (115) Edward F. Skinner, **For King and Country**; (116) James Prinsep Beadle, **Zero Hour**; (117) Sir David Cameron, **The Battlefield of Ypres**; (135) Colin U. Gill, **The Captive**; (136) David Bomberg, **Sappers at Work**; (145) John Nash, **Over the Top**; (146/7) Georges Leroux, **L'Enfer**; (148 top) Paul Nash, **The Mule Track**; (148 bottom) Harold Sandys Williamson, **The Route Nationale**; (157) P. Wyndham Lewis, **A Battery Position in a Wood**; (158) Gilbert Rogers, **The Dead Stretcher-Bearer**; (175) C. R. W. Nevinson, **The Road from Arras to Bapaume**; (176) Paul Nash, **Spring in the Trenches, Ridge Wood 1917**. The Mary Evans Picture Library: (17), (75), (78), (96). E. T. Archive: (118).

BLACK & WHITE ILLUSTRATIONS

The Trustees of the Imperial War Museum: (2), (24), (56), (85), (88), (101), (153), (168). The Mary Evans Picture Library: (3), (11), (38), (39), (53), (67), (83), (87), (109), (110), (125), (129), (137), (150), (155), (171), (172), (173). National Portrait Gallery: (16), (28), (138), (166), (177), (178). Illustrated London News Picture Library: (9), (20). BBC Hulton Picture Library: (25), (27), (63), (86), (127), (142–3), (167). Reproduced by permission of Punch: (1), (91), (149), (164). The Mansell Collection: (9), (26), (151). Peter Lawrence: (22), (29), (44), (70), (93), (133), (140), (152), (186). Peter Newark's Historical Pictures: (59), (89), (103). Weidenfeld & Nicolson Library & Archives: (49). BPCC/Aldus Archive: (141). E.T. Archive: (154). John Frost: (5), (33), (50), (61), (112), (163).

POETRY

BY PERMISSION OF: Macmillan, London & Basingstoke & Mr Michael Gibson/W. W. Gibson *Collected Poems 1905–25*; Macmillan/Osbert Sitwell *Selected Satires and Poems*; the Estate of Ford Madox Ford and Bodley Head/*Bodley Head Ford Madox Ford*; reprinted by permission of Faber & Faber Ltd./Herbert Read *Collected Poems*, and *Siegfried Sassoon: Diaries 1915–1918* edited by Rupert Hart-Davis; Gollancz/Edith Sitwell *Clown's Houses*; Michael Hamburger/poems from *George Trakl: A Profile* (Carcanet) and *German Poetry 1910–1975* (Carcanet); A. P. Watt Ltd. on behalf of the executors of the Estate of Robert Graves; Oxford University Press/ Michael Hurd *The Ordeal of Ivor Gurney*, *Collected Letters* edited by Harold Owen and John Bell, Jon Stallworthy *Wilfred Owen: A Biography*, *The Oxford Book of Modern Verse 1892–1935*; © Robin Haines, sole trustee of the Gurney Estate 1982. Reprinted from *Collected Poems of Ivor Gurney* edited by P. J. Kavanagh (1982) by permission of Oxford University Press; Unwin Human Ltd./Richard Aldington *Collected Poems*, Tim Travers *The Killing Ground*, Margaret Postgate Cole *Collected Poems*; © 1922 by Holt, Rinehart & Winston, Inc., © 1950 by Barclays Bank Ltd., reprinted from *Collected Poems of A. E. Housman* by permission of Henry Holt & Company, Inc.; Anvil Press Poetry/*Apollinaire Selected Poems* trans. Oliver Bernard 1986; John Murray (Publishers) Ltd./*Winifred M. Letts Halloween and other Poems*; Edmund Blunden *Undertones of War* reprinted by permission of A. D. Peters & Co. Ltd.; Patrick Bridgwater/Lichtenstein's "Leaving for the Front", Stramm's "Guard-duty"; Jonathan Griffin/Ungaretti's "Vigil" and "Brothers"; Hodder & Stoughton/May Sinclair's "Field Ambulance in Retreat" from *King Albert's Book*; Trustees of the Imperial War Museum/George Coppard *With a Machine Gun to Cambrai*; David McDuff/Stadler's "Decampment"; Myfanwy Thomas/Edward Thomas *Collected Poems*; Dodd, Mead & Company, Inc./*The Collected Poems of G. K. Chesterton* © 1932 Dodd, Mead & Company, Inc. © renewed 1959 by Oliver Chesterton; Thames & Hudson/John Lehman *Poets of the First World War*; Anthony Sheil Associates/ Martin Seymour Smith *Robert Graves His Life & Work*; by permission of Mrs Nicolete Gray and The Society of Authors on behalf of the Laurence Binyon Estate; Peter Newbolt/ *Henry Newbolt Collected Poems*; George Sassoon/*Siegfried Sassoon Collected Poems 1908–1956*; Carcanet Press/Edgell Rickword *Behind the Eyes; Collected Poems and Selected Translations*; Collins/Margaret Postgate Cole's "The Veteran" from *An Anthology of War Poems*; Constable/Walter de la Mare *Collected Verse*, Rose Macaulay *Three Days*; Harcourt Brace Jovanovitch/*Sandburg Complete Poems*; Houghton Mifflin/Florence Ripley Mastin's "At the Movies" from *A Treasury of War Poetry*; Christopher Middleton/Ehrenstein's "The Poet and War"; Schocken Books Inc./*Isaac Rosenberg Collected Poems* ed. Bottomley & Harding; Alan Sutton Publishing Ltd./John Laffin *On the Western Front*; Sidgwick & Jackson Ltd./Herbert Asquith *Poems 1912–1933*, F. W. Harvey *Gloucestershire Friends*; Chatto & Windus/Robert Nichols *Ardours and Endurances, The Poems of Wilfred Owen* edited by Jon Stallworthy, Julian Grenfell's "Into Battle" from *Men Who March Away*; Vera Brittain's poems "Perhaps . . .", "The Lament of the Demobilised", and "To My Brother" from *Testament of Youth* are included with the permission of her literary executors.